T0077898

CARE FOR
THE DYING

A Practical Biblical Guide for
Ministering to People Who Are Terminally Ill

CHAPLAIN TOM

WESTBOW
PRESS®
A DIVISION OF THOMAS NELSON
& ZONDERVAN

WestBow Press books may be ordered through booksellers or by contacting:

WestBow Press
A Division of Thomas Nelson & Zondervan
1663 Liberty Drive
Bloomington, IN 47403
www.westbowpress.com
1 (866) 928-1240

ISBN: 978-1-9736-1248-3 (sc)
ISBN: 978-1-9736-1247-6 (e)

Print information available on the last page.

WestBow Press rev. date: 01/08/2018

FOREWORD

My Dad was diagnosed with cancer that probably began in his pancreas but had spread though out his abdomen. He needed a hospice service and I immediately chose a hospice only because I knew they had a chaplain that was my friend.

Chaplain Tom has been a friend for over 20 years. I knew him to be a man with a heart of compassion and a tremendous desire to help those who are going through difficult times. I knew I needed a friend as I faced the reality that my Dad had terminal cancer and would not live very long. On Thanksgiving Day fourteen years ago my Dad died and there to help me was my friend Chaplain Tom. I will never forget what a blessing he was to me and my family.

In this insightful book he shares how to minister to those who are sick and dying. Everyone can gain wisdom from the powerful experiences that Tom shares from real life situations. No one can really live life at its best until we know how to face death. We have all struggled to know what to say during these difficult times. Chaplain Tom shares practical ways to effectively help those facing the reality of death. I wish I could have read a book like this forty years ago. It is long overdue! Thank you Chaplain Tom!

Pastor Bill

PREFACE

While serving as co-pastor of a small church in a big city I got a disturbing phone call. One of the ladies who regularly came to our church was in the hospital. The physicians had determined that this lady (we will call her Kim.) had an ovarian tumor. The plan was to do surgery in order to remove the tumor, as well as one or both of her ovaries. Kim was facing a problem that could very possibly be a terminal disease. She was also still of child-bearing age but had never borne a child. This added to the heartache and anxiety.

It was my responsibility to go and visit this dear lady in the hospital before she went into surgery. What if you got this call? What is one to do? What was I supposed to say at a time like this? I had little idea what to do or what to say. I was not prepared and I was afraid to make this visit. The hospital setting was a little scary. The devastating possibilities of this diagnosis were rather overwhelming. I knew I should go. I knew I should pray. I did both, and that was probably about all that I got right that day.

I will not leave you wondering what happened to Kim. The surgery was completed and, thank God, the suspected tumor turned out to be a benign cyst that was completely removed. One ovary was saved, and Kim recovered well.

Several years later, on a Friday night, I was working admissions in the ER waiting area at a local hospital. I had gone back to school, working on a seminary degree and earning my way by doing a paperwork job at the hospital. A man in his forties came running into the waiting area, desperately asking where he could find his wife. I did not know what was happening, but soon found out that his wife had just minutes earlier arrived at the ER in an ambulance. I had only brief contact with the very distraught man before he was directed back into the ER itself. Soon one of the staff members almost tearfully reported to me and others that this man's wife had apparently had a heart attack, and the prognosis did not look good at all.

I desperately wanted to go and be of some help to this man and his wife. I knew at that point it was really not my job to do so, and then I began to realize that I really would not even know how to be a help to them. I earnestly wanted to be able to reach out to them somehow. I anxiously continued with the paperwork I had to do, which seemed so meaningless at that moment. Then word came up to our desk that this patient, the wife of the desperate man, had died. I was swept with such intense emotions of sorrow and frustration with my own inability to do anything for them. I prayed for this man and his family, and I also prayed that somehow I could be of help the next time. A few days later, as I looked at a bulletin board at the hospital, I read something about openings for chaplains in their new CPE program. That stands for clinical pastoral education, which is a type of "on the job training" for those preparing to be chaplains. Through some amazing events, I was very soon able to quit my paperwork job at the hospital and began what became three semesters of CPE. I was also able to complete my Master of Divinity degree before beginning my last semester as a resident chaplain.

I have often recommended at least a semester or two of CPE for those preparing to go into ministry. I realize that relatively few actually take such an opportunity. I was told many times that nothing else could begin to replace the kind of training and experience that one gets from actually working in a hospital in such an intense training program. That is probably true, but I have had a strong desire for several years now to somehow share with others what I have learned through my own experiences, both in CPE and then working for many more years with patients who are terminally ill.

With this book, my hope is to pass along to you some practical principles and guidelines that will help you as you minister to people who are sick or dying. These same instructions will help you as you minister to their families and friends as well.

Throughout this book, I will repeatedly refer to the Bible and to my own experiences.

Please listen graciously and thoughtfully. Please don't be too quick to say to yourself, "Oh, I already get that." One important topic that will be majored on is the essential art of really listening to those we minister to.

I readily confess that as a chaplain intern, I was in some respects a slow learner. Sometimes the slow learner can be a more effective teacher than the guy who just seems to get it all the first time around. My Dad actually helped me to see this when he talked to me about his own career in the Air Force. Dad said that the mission he had been most successful at was teaching others how to fly helicopters. He told me he had not been the quickest or the best student pilot himself. He said that most often, the Air Force tended to pick the quickest learners to become their flight instructors, and he felt that was a mistake. He actually was a better instructor because he had to struggle with the learning process himself.

The harsh reality is that every person to whom we minister will one day be sick or dying. It is often the case that people will look to a Christian minister for the first time, or for the first time in a long time, when they are diagnosed with a serious or a terminal illness. I want you to be equipped to be there for them. I hope that the reading of this book will take away much of the mystery and most of the fear that you might have in this regard.

I will share enough stories to keep this interesting and, more importantly, to keep it real.

I have prayerfully tried to be concise in these pages. Hopefully a simple "you and I" format will serve well here. This is really not about Systematic Theology, but I hope you might learn something more about God's heart and about human hearts as well.

PEGS

<u>Principles</u>:
- About <u>you</u>: Understand who you are. Be real. Really be doing what God requires of you.
- Meet <u>the Patient</u> where he is.
- Depend on <u>God</u> to do what only He can do.

<u>Essentials</u> to do:
- Respect everyone
- Listen intentionally
- Journey With
- Choose to Love

<u>Guidelines</u> to follow
- Don't point to the silver lining.
- Don't say, "I understand."
- Don't be in a hurry.
- Don't step on hope.
- Don't immediately shoot down the patient's belief system.
- Be cautious with humor.
- Be generous with affirmation.
- Hear confessions.
- Keep your message simple.
- Be a rock, not a landslide.
- Deal with discouragement.
- Do not be a "respecter of persons."

<u>Situations</u> to consider – (based on real scenarios)
- Situations according to place:
  1. In a hospital room
  2. In an ICU
  3. In the ER
  4. In a nursing or rehabilitation facility
  5. In a private home

"Grace to you and peace from God our Father and the Lord Jesus Christ.

I thank my God upon every remembrance of you,

always in every prayer of mine making request for you all with joy,

for your fellowship in the Gospel from the first day until now,

being confident of this very thing, that He who has begun a good work in you will complete it until the day of Jesus Christ;

just as it is right for me to think this of you all, because I have you in my heart, inasmuch as both in my chains and in the defense and confirmation of the Gospel, you all are partakers with me of grace.

For God is my witness, how greatly I long for you all with the affection of Jesus Christ.

And this I pray, that your love may abound still more and more in knowledge and all discernment,

that you may approve the things that are excellent, that you may be sincere and without offense till the day of Christ,

being filled with the fruits of righteousness which are by Jesus Christ, to the glory and praise of God."

Philippians 1:3-11

THREE PRINCIPLES

I

ABOUT YOU

(IN GENERAL)

There are always at least three involved in every visit with a patient. They are you, the one you minister to, and the Lord Himself. The Lord is always there, ready to work in your heart, and in the heart of your patient. We have three to consider here; I would like to start with you and save the Best for last.

Since you have picked up this book, I am presuming that you want God to use you to help others in their times of need. If you are anything like me, you have found yourself wanting to help someone, but wishing you knew more about what to do and what to say. Maybe you have found yourself afraid of doing or saying the wrong thing. It means a lot just to have the desire to be a comforter, a peacemaker, or just a blessing to someone else. It is a great blessing simply to be used by God to encourage another.

When you see longer passages from Scripture in these pages, please do not hurry through the verses, even when you recognize them as being familiar. Please let God's Word speak to you.

1 Corinthians 1:26-31 reads as follows:
"For you see your calling, brethren, that not many wise according to the flesh, not many mighty, not many noble, are called. But God has chosen the foolish things of the world to put to shame the wise, and God has chosen the weak things of the world to put to shame the things which are mighty; and the base things of the world and the things which are despised

God has chosen, and the things which are not, to bring to nothing the things that are, that no flesh should glory in His presence. But of Him you are in Christ Jesus, who became for us wisdom from God—and righteousness and sanctification and redemption—that, as it is written, "He who glories, let him glory in the LORD."

Now, let's reflect here just a bit. Some want to discuss whether the "called" in these verses are all of the children of God or just all those called into some particular service for God. Either way, this is talking about you and me. We are the weak and the foolish. We are humans with many limitations and God chooses to use us anyway. He actually delights in using us; the ones who are weak and foolish. It shows just how great He is! That really takes a lot of pressure off of you and me. We do not have to be strong or brilliant. And think about how great this whole plan is for us; it is like a great coach taking over an underperforming high school team, taking them all the way to the State championship and winning. Who gets the glory? The coach does! The same players did poorly before the new coach arrived. Now, together, they are champions.

It is truly great to be on this coach's team. It is wonderful to be a part of achieving great things. It's like Gideon and his band of 300 men defeating tens of thousands of Midianites using just trumpets and torches. It's like the handful of fishermen and a few other ordinary guys, who spent three years with Jesus, then went out and changed the entire world with His message of redemption and hope. It's like the barely-educated shoe salesman, Dwight Moody, who became a faithful Sunday school teacher and then went on to preach all across this country and England and Scotland, winning untold numbers to Christ. "He who glories, let him glory in the LORD."

Again, look how great this is for us. We get to play for, and work on, Team Jesus. In earlier days, we may not have even made the junior varsity team, but here we are playing for the greatest coach of all time, on the greatest team that ever took the field. God loves you and has chosen to use you. And by the way, you were not the last one chosen either.

You might have noticed that the last verse in the 1 Corinthians passage above was referring to a statement elsewhere in Scripture. Let's read Jeremiah 9:23-24.

Thus says the LORD:
"Let not the wise *man* glory in his wisdom, Let not the mighty *man* glory in his might, Nor let the rich *man* glory in his riches; But let him who glories glory in this, That he understands and knows Me, That I am the LORD, exercising loving kindness, judgment, and righteousness in the earth. For in these I delight," says the LORD.

Wow! I find that to be a powerful message. Now let's focus on the first of three points that are for and about you.

A. We should **understand who we are**.

Each one of us is very much human and we have significant limitations. So consider our humanity for a moment here. We do not walk on water. We can't fly. We can't lift even a small sub-compact car. Now, if you read these words and were thinking of ways you could possibly do these things, (if you just had the right tools), then you might need to seriously reflect on this reality. There is so much more we cannot do than there are things that we can do. Jesus gave us some very memorable words in John 15:5, "for without Me you can do nothing." Speaking of His own dependence on the Father during His earthly ministry, Jesus said in John 5:30, "I can of Myself do nothing." Yes, we can scoot things around, basically rearranging our own furnishings. We can speak a bunch of our own words, but on our own, we really cannot accomplish anything.

Even when we do get right in the middle of God's wonderful plan, and He actually works through us to accomplish great things, God is still going to use a number of other people along with us. This is because we really are little humans with big limitations.

Now, please forgive me, and allow me to say a few words about the not so lovely side of our basic humanity. I remember during clinical pastoral education in our local hospital, we had been talking about what it means

3

to be human. We had discussed being stuck in and dependent on these frail, temporary, dirty, mortal bodies. Well, I had been eating some great, spicy Mexican food from the hospital cafeteria. The time came for me to do what all of us humans do on a regular basis. There was a rather small public bathroom in the basement of the hospital, and while I was still in the only stall, a man began to walk through the bathroom door. His nose smelled what I had done. He loudly said, "Oh, *Expletive!*" and walked out. I laughed out loud and said to myself, "Well, I guess I'm human too." Human we are and human are all of your patients. We all urinate and defecate. We all pass gas. We all stink when we are not bathed regularly. We are all born incontinent and in our final days, most of us will be incontinent again. We all have bodies that grow old, fail us in so many ways, and then die. Of course, God knows all of this and He loves us anyway

B. We need to **Be Real**.

We need to be honest. We need to be real. We need to be authentic. This is foundational because God insists that we be honest. There is one thing we are told clearly in Scripture that God cannot do. God cannot lie. Read Titus 1:2. It is an interesting reality that even people who do not claim to have any religious inclinations insist that we be honest with them. I am convinced that people have always wanted this from others. Even today, the same individuals who champion relativism are still seen demanding honesty from us in our dealings with them; especially if their time or their money is involved. Cheating and fraud may be on the rise, but the people we meet every day still have little tolerance for anyone who is not real and honest with them. People still want to be able to trust someone. Many people are hoping you will be that person whom they can trust. It is also essential that we be kind and gracious. We will get to that part soon enough, but as important as kindness is, we first need to be real.

To try to express what I mean by being real, perhaps it will help to look at a personal example of not being real.

When I first started as a chaplain intern, we were told to write out some goals that we hoped to accomplish during our first semester of "on the job training" at the hospital. As one of my goals, I wrote something about how I wanted to learn how to act, speak and dress so that patients and hospital staff would respect me and listen to me. Jay (our supervisor) was patient with me. It took a little while, but I realized that this goal of mine was all about *me*, and others looking at and listening to *me*. It was completely turned in the wrong direction. I did not realize it at the time, but I was focusing on *myself*. I wanted to know how I could ACT IN SUCH A WAY that others would think more *of me*, so they would listen *to me*. The hospital patients did not need me to act in any such way. They needed me to be real. They also needed me to focus on them, and they needed me to do the listening.

The truth is that people don't think all that much of actors. They want someone who will be real with them, someone they can trust.

I am sure you are not hearing this theme for the first time. We rather frequently hear admonitions to be authentic. I hope you have heard such messages. I am fully on board with being authentic. I feel the need, however, to encourage some thoughtful consideration on this subject. Our modern western society often spends so much time and effort focusing on the individual that it sometimes goes overboard. Here is a story from my life that might help you reflect on your own perspective.

While still in my twenties, I headed off to a new field of ministry in Europe. I sincerely asked a veteran pastor, "How should I act toward these people that I am going to serve?" I remember being told to, "Just be yourself." I am certain that at that point I did not fully understand what the pastor was trying to tell me. I invite you to reflect with me on how we can better define what being authentic could mean. I have searched for a long time now, but have not found any instruction in the Bible that says "just be yourself."

The Lord chose Abraham, but he did not tell him, "Just be yourself." God worked for a few decades in Abraham's life before he eventually became a great example of a man of faith. David was called a man after God's own heart, but I do not read that God told David, "just be yourself." God brought David through all kinds of adversity and worked hard on David's rough edges. On one occasion, when David was clearly just being himself, he dove into adultery and murder. We read in all four Gospels about how Jesus taught his apostles, but I have never read a line about Jesus telling any of them, "Just be yourselves." The Patriarchs, the best of the Kings and Prophets, the Apostles and Pastors and Deacons apparently all needed to be molded and shaped into the persons God wanted them to be.

I would like to clearly warn against excusing ourselves from the demands of Scripture by falling back on a popular theme of, "I just have to be myself," or even by saying, "Oh, this is just the way God made me." God did purposefully make you, in many ways, to be unique from all others. But as long as we are still breathing, God is still working on us. Paul told the Philippians in Chapter 1 verse 6 that he was "…confident of this very thing, that He who has begun a good work in you will complete it until the day of Jesus Christ."

I have come to believe that the intended message of that sincere pastor who spoke to me long ago was this: be honest, do not try to be something you are not and do not be a hypocrite. At the same time, I would also like to point out that there is no doubt that the people in Europe did not really need to see me; not even a most sincere me. But wouldn't it be wonderful for these people to see a reflection of Jesus Christ in me?

The best thing you and I can possibly do with our words and actions is to reflect the character and love of Christ. This concept is as old as the early days of the Church at Antioch, where they were first called "Christians" (Acts 11:26). Being a Christian has always been about being Christ-like. I am sure that this principle will never change.

Asking and allowing God to shape us into who He wants us to be is in no way averse to being authentic. It just means we want God to keep working in our hearts and lives so we can eventually become all that He wants us to be.

This is a lot of what the somewhat difficult and certainly challenging verses in Philippians 3:7-14 are all about. Verses 8-10 read "…I also count all things loss for the excellence of the knowledge of Christ Jesus my Lord, for whom I have suffered the loss of all things, and count them as rubbish, that I may gain Christ and be found in Him, not having my own righteousness, which is from the law, but that which is through faith in Christ, the righteousness which is from God by faith; that I may know Him and the power of His resurrection, and the fellowship of His sufferings, being conformed to His death."

Please hear the challenging example of Paul in verses 12 and 14: "I press on, that I may lay hold of that for which Christ Jesus has also laid hold of me. … I press toward the goal for the prize of the upward call of God in Christ Jesus."

I'm pretty simple minded, so I like the picture of that little child wearing the t-shirt that says, "God's still working on me." I am confident that He is still working on me, and on you too.

A big part of being authentic is accepting the way that God has made us. We do well to learn to accept and even embrace our own specific abilities and our limitations.

Some would encourage you to charge out on a quest in the desert or the mountains to "find yourself." The answers are usually not there. I remember as a teenager imagining what kind of ministry God might use me in. Once I thought I might be the next Billy Graham, preaching to tens of thousands in huge stadiums. Young people often imagine themselves to be superheroes. Even those who do become "superheroes" generally have to start with small things. I would encourage you to speak with your local church pastor. Share your heart for ministry and ask if he can show you possible places where you can serve Christ now. Seek out a place to serve with others who might have more experience and are currently serving faithfully. While actively serving the Lord, we tend to learn what our God-given gifts and abilities really are.

So, in summation: Be real. Be determined to become the person God made you to be. Ask and freely allow the Lord Himself to keep on shaping you into the person He wants you to be. Purposefully work at imitating Christ and follow others who serve Him faithfully.

C. We should be determined to be **doing what God requires us to do**.

The basis for this third little section is one simple, yet profound verse: Micah 6:8 "He has shown you, O man what is good; And what does the LORD require of you but to:

- Do justly. Be honest, be fair, be loyal, do not harm, or steal from, or be envious of others.
- Love mercy. Receive mercy and give mercy to others, just as God has given mercy to you. Be kind, be gracious.
- Walk humbly with your God. The only way to truly walk with God is to do so with a humble attitude.

"Do justly" These two words are about as basic and broad as anything we could imagine. Please do not hurry past what appears to be too simple or what appears to be simply impossible. Micah was really not proclaiming anything new with these words and I certainly do not want to either. When Micah said these words to the people of Jerusalem, he was appealing to what they already knew. When they heard these words, their minds hopefully went straight to the Word of God that had already been given to them. Our minds should also go there. If we go forth as ministers of the Gospel, those to whom we minister will expect us to follow directions that God has clearly given to us.

"Love mercy" Many years ago I was filling in for another pastor in a small village church near a city in the western part of Germany. It was a Saturday afternoon when I started to walk up a road leading to the edge of the village. I saw an older man pass by me, heading downhill on his bicycle. I did not see what happened, but I heard the disturbing sound. Quickly turning around, I saw that the man had fallen from his bicycle and was

lying on the ground, momentarily unconscious from the impact. A couple of other pedestrians got to the man just before I did, and someone dutifully called 110 (the German equivalent of 911). It took only a few minutes for a uniformed police officer to arrive at the scene.

The officer stood near the fallen man, never bending down, never touching the man. He pulled out a pen and notepad and began writing down what had happened. Out loud the officer said, "There is obviously some sand on the road here and this man was going too fast down the hill. When he applied the brakes of his bicycle, he slid and fell. He should not have been going so fast and should have been more cautious."

Moments later another man arrived carrying a medical bag. He lived just a few doors down from this location, and he was an emergency medical technician. More precisely, his main occupation was to train others to be EMT's. He also attended the church where I was filling in for the pastor. While the law officer had made no attempt to help the fallen man, he did speak words that were undeniably true. He recorded accurately what had happened, but he had no immediate help to give. He was the law.

The neighbor/EMT had a completely different approach to the ugly scene on the road that day. He hurried to the fallen man's side as soon as he heard of his need. He quickly assessed the man's injuries and his physical condition. He cleaned and bandaged an obvious injury on the man's forehead and placed the man in a safe position until he could be lifted from the ground and placed into an ambulance.

This kind, helpful man did not ask for the injured man's credentials. He did not ask where he had come from. This gentle soul did not seem to care how the fallen man had been injured; he just wanted to help him with the knowledge and skills that he had.

The officer and the EMT dramatically pictured law and mercy in a way that I will never forget.

When we fall, each of us needs and almost always appreciates mercy. It is normal and natural to gladly receive almost any gesture of mercy. I do not think, however, that this is the primary message that Micah has for us. That would almost be too easy. We need to see that mercy travels in both directions. As we receive mercy, we need to know that we are also expected to give mercy.

I remember visiting an elderly religious man who was terminally ill. He told me he found it best to pray the Lord's Prayer when he prayed, so I was glad to pray this great model prayer with him. After just a few visits, when we had built some level of trust, he told me that he really struggled with the part about forgiving those who have trespassed against us. I replied that, unfortunately, I had some difficult news for him. I showed him the next two verses that come right after the Lord's Prayer in Matthew 6:9-13. I pointed and he read, "For if you forgive men their trespasses, your heavenly Father will also forgive you. But if you do not forgive men their trespasses, neither will your Father forgive your trespasses." The man appeared to be hit hard by these words, but he did receive them and I think he began to understand what mercy really was.

One of the highest and most noble demands upon us as followers of Christ is that we extend mercy and grace, even to those whom we see as unworthy of such. Sometimes, without even noticing, we can become tight-fisted with our hold on mercy and forgiveness. I believe the only real cure for this is to continually keep in our minds the mercy that Christ gave to us. Remember that we are, in fact, just as much in need of God's mercy as anyone we might visit, whether in a filthy little house, a county hospital, a state prison or a three-million-dollar home. We should love mercy, delight in it and long to share it with the least deserving we might encounter.

"Walk humbly with your God." I see humility as a clear realization of one's own true position and one's own limitations. The truth is that you and I often tend to think that we are better than we are. We also tend to think that we are more humble than we really are.

When I was a young college student, I thought I was just that — pretty humble. Then as I struggled through graduate school, I actually did become a little more humble, as I realized that I was not as smart as I had thought

I was. Then after teaching for a couple of years and becoming the father of two children, I realized that I was not nearly as capable as I wanted to be. Then we were off to Europe, trying to help plant a new church in a large city, and I had to recognize that I really was way in over my head.

Looking back, I think my experiences were certainly enough to produce a lot of humility in anybody. It is amazing how I could manage to hang onto so much pride in the midst of difficult struggles and clear demonstrations of my own shortcomings. I have come to see that most of us have a hard time letting go of pride, no matter what reality has to show us. I have also seen that failure and loss were things that eventually brought me to a clearer understanding of what humility might actually be.

Even in the midst of failure, our own inward pride can stubbornly keep on fighting through. We tend to justify or excuse our own failures, coming up with some external reason for why we failed. We end up thinking, "It was someone else's fault after all." We usually view the failures of others differently, more objectively, than we view our own.

Some wise person noted that we rarely measure others with the same ruler that we use to measure ourselves. Falling short of my own expectations as a pastor, and failing in other ways as a Dad, has humbled me. I never wanted to be humbled in those ways, but here I am and there is nothing glorious about it. Glorious it is not, but good it is.

The Lord uses Peter to give us this magnificent invitation in 1 Peter 5:5-7: "Likewise you younger people, submit yourselves to your elders. Yes, all of you be submissive to one another, and be clothed with humility, for *God resists the proud, but gives grace to the humble.* Therefore humble yourselves under the mighty hand of God, that He may exalt you in due time, *casting all your care upon Him for He cares for you.*"

The sentence at the end of verse 5 about how God reacts to the proud and to the humble, is a reference to Proverbs 3:34, and is also found in James 4:6.

Please allow me another observation here. Just as we tend to overestimate our own humility, we also tend to see some of our own behaviors as evidence of humility when they might actually be symptoms of something very different. I am going way back for a moment to my high school days. I played doubles on my school's tennis team. That sounds pretty humble, doesn't it? But apparently, I thought I was a better tennis player than I actually was. When I missed shots that I was sure I could hit or when I would double fault on a serve, I got angry. Since I was angry at myself, I thought I was being humble. The truth is just the opposite. A humble athlete would simply say, "I have missed that shot before. I really should practice more than I do." Or he might say, "My opponent is clearly better than I am."

The humble person is neither surprised nor is he angry when he fails at something. The proud person is both: surprised and angry. All of my anger at myself was simple pride. Problems with my hips keep me from playing tennis today, but I sometimes wonder how much more I could enjoy the game now. I like to think that I can now much better accept who I am and what my own limitations are.

It is surely a good thing to try to do our best at whatever we are called upon to do and to ask God for help. I have to ask, however, do you sometimes lose your temper in your favorite competitive pursuits? Again, humility does not cause us to lose our temper, pride does. The vast majority of anger that we see in others, and experience in ourselves, comes from pride. Frankly, I am embarrassed to think how long it took me to realize that my anger at my own failings was, and occasionally still is, nothing but sinful pride.

Sometimes we find ourselves wanting to show others that we really are humble. That usually means we are "acting humble." It is good if we can begin to arrive at a place where we truly see ourselves as no better than those we work with or those we minister to. When I do see myself as being no better than those I minister to, I do not have to *act* humble.

Humility is really very appealing. A humble person can rest in the strength and ability of others. A humble person does not have to be independent and self-sufficient.

Almost everyone would rather spend time with a humble person than with a proud person. Someone who is sick or dying would almost certainly rather spend his limited time with a person who is humble. Humility is all positive. It is not averse, in any way, to wisdom or courage or even boldness and assertiveness. Humility makes us more able to properly embrace these other qualities. We will bring up the topic of humility again when we talk specifically about how to be a good listener.

I have come to see that many times, perhaps even most of the times, when we are not truly authentic; it is because we are fearful. Many of us find ourselves afraid of what other people may be thinking about us. I think we can all remember occasions when we were trying to *act like* we were not afraid, or maybe even trying to *act like* we knew what we were doing? Perhaps you have been afraid to knock on a door, make a phone call, or speak a needed word. Maybe you went ahead and did what you knew you should do, but you were fearful in the doing of it. If so, then you are right here with many of the rest of us.

There is an appendix to this book that has some words to say about fear. I did not put it back there because it is not important. I decided to put it in a section all to itself because it was afraid of the other chapters. There I go trying to be funny. I actually wrote this appendix on the problem of fear because I have had plenty of experience with it, and I feel it is very important to confront it. God has given me clear personal victories in this realm, and I want to try and share with you what I have experienced and learned. If you want to go ahead and read this appendix before you start with this next section, go ahead. I won't even try to stop you.

Flee also youthful lusts; but pursue righteousness, faith, love, peace with those who call on the Lord out of a pure heart.

But avoid foolish and ignorant disputes, knowing that they generate strife.

And a servant of the Lord must not quarrel but be gentle to all, able to teach, patient,

in humility correcting those who are in opposition, if God perhaps will grant them repentance, so that they may know the truth,

and that they may come to their senses and escape the snare of the devil, having been taken captive by him to do his will.

2 Timothy 2:22-26

II

LET THE PATIENT BE HIMSELF

Work at recognizing who the one **is** that you are called upon to minister **to**. Try to figure out where he is on his journey and meet him there.

Paul writes in 1 Corinthians 9:22 "to the weak I became as weak, that I might win the weak. I have become all things to all men; that I might by all means save some."

This is a very important principle: As much as possible, we also should work at becoming all things to each person we minister to. But how do we even know **who** this person really is? How do you know **where** he is on his journey?

The answer is simple enough: Look, Listen *and, when necessary*, Ask.

When I first began as a chaplain intern, I thought I would do just great with people. I had a thousand great stories to tell. I had lived in over a dozen places, met fascinating people, read lots of history, and even experienced a lot of history. I have seen some things that others only dream of seeing. Well, guess what? All those things have only occasionally helped me a little in ministering to others. More often, my desire to tell my own stories to others has actually hurt my ability to minister to them.

We can easily fall into the practice of trying to match, or even to top, each of our patient's stories with one of our own. People who need help, people who are hurting physically, emotionally or spiritually, very rarely need to hear our interesting stories. *That may be shocking, but it's true.* But, **I felt a need to tell my own story**... (I still slip into that occasionally).

The point that I earnestly want to make is that people who are hurting and people who are dying have a need. ***They need to tell their own story.*** They are longing to meet someone who truly wants to listen to them. You and I can be that person.

> *Now I would like to note that I realize I am telling you lots of stories. This is because I am writing as a teacher. Stories and parables can be valuable teaching tools, but grieving people do not need to be taught nearly as much as they need to be heard. They need someone to be there for them. They don't so much need an instructor as they need someone to care for their souls.*

Here is a great key to ministry. A chaplain, a minister or any other person can **simply listen** to the one in need, the one in a mess, the one going through grief. Only the one in need really knows what he or she is going through and what has happened in his or her life. Certainly, God knows, but who else could possibly be able to gain insight into what this person is going through? **Anyone who is prepared to listen.**

It is a simple, amazing reality. If there is a gracious and willing listener present, the one in need will eventually eventually go through a process of putting his situation and his needs into words. This requires some thinking, some organization of thoughts, and usually some sense of chronology and priority on the patient's part.

Most of the time in this process, the one in need will:

- Make some sense of what is going on in his life
- Will often come to some sort of answers and conclusions

When he does this:

- Good conclusions can be affirmed by the listener
- Poor or dangerous conclusions can be respectfully questioned by the listener

Even if the patient comes to <u>no conclusions</u> in the sharing of his story, there are generally still two positive results:

1. You (the listener) will have received some information that will likely be helpful.
2. The one in need will now be more ready and willing to listen to guidance from you because you are the one who listened to him or her. *People almost always appreciate and value someone who listens to them.*

I learned these basic principles while doing my clinical pastoral education in a local hospital. The process was not given in the above points or even put in any kind of outline, but these simple steps are a big part of what my experience in the hospital taught me. This has remained an important part of how I have ministered to people for many years.

I would like to add an important note to this principle of meeting people where they are. While you are watching and listening to the patient; ***be cautious about giving hints of holy expectations.*** Most people pick up a lot from our expressions and body language in addition to our words. Sometimes a patient will begin to share something that could be shocking, and he or she will quickly see if you are shocked. If you immediately appear to be judgmental of what he tells you, he probably will stop right there and keep the rest to himself.

Experience has taught me to calmly expect shocking things. However, when *I am shocked and it shows*, I have learned to just say, "Wow." Or even, "Wow, I'm a little shocked here." You could then follow that up with something like, "But, I really want to understand what that was like for you." Again, it is important to ***be honest*** and to ***be real***.

It also does not help if your appearance is a little too other-worldly. To meet someone where he is, it helps if we look like someone with whom he can feel comfortable. Avoid extremes. It's better not to stand out in the crowd. I rarely wear suits and ties, except where and when they are clearly appropriate. I have two nice funeral suits. I almost always wear one of them when I officiate, and sometimes when I attend a funeral. I very rarely wear a suit when visiting people in their homes or in a facility. Again, a huge part of letting the patient **be** who he is, is meeting him **where** he is.

If a person is clearly not well educated, we don't need to use some fancy college vocabulary on him. I think we can all speak simply and directly. Please don't patronize. Don't say, "I know you may not understand this, but I'll make it simple." Keep it simple but don't suggest to the patient that you think he is simple. "God is sovereign and omniscient," becomes, "God is still in control and He knows what you're going through." Strangely, it sometimes takes a few more words to say things simply.

A good question is almost always more effective than a declarative statement. Think about how many questions Jesus asked people, even though He already knew all the answers. It really is good for us to avoid making a lot of grand statements. They make us sound like we think we are "know-it-alls." (Perhaps you remember Cliff — the postman on the 1980's TV show "Cheers." If I'm not careful, I can be that guy.) It is important for the patient to see that you really are interested in him and that you really care. Also, be cautious not to use so many questions that the patient begins to feel as if he is being interrogated. Freely give the patient the right to his or her privacy. It's very good to give a person an open door to share, but be cautious with probing questions.

You remember the good old saying, ***"They don't care how much you know until they know how much you care."*** This really is a "good old saying" that is worth embracing and applying. Don't just ***tell*** the patient that you value him; ***show him*** by listening to him.

It is helpful to notice that Jesus did not speak to the woman at the well (John 4), the same way that he spoke to Nicodemus (John 3). He did not speak to Zacchaeus (Luke 19) the same way that he spoke to the centurion (Matthew 8). Jesus did not even speak to two sisters the same way in the same situation in the same 11th chapter of John. Jesus spoke in different ways to different people because He knew that each of their hearts and minds were different. He knew they had their own particular needs. Well, you might say, He is Jesus. How can I know my patient's heart and mind? How can I know his needs?

You know the answer: Look, Listen and, when necessary, Ask.

I want to give what should be an obvious warning. Do not jump to conclusions too quickly. Please do not decide that you know all about a patient just by his or her appearance. Certainly do not assume you know something about his head or his heart, based on the clothes he wears or on his race or even his cultural background. Listening to what your patient has to say is the best way to learn about him. There have been times when I was surprised, even shocked, when I listened and realized that the person I was looking at was not at all the kind of person I had thought he was.

I recently met a lady who was a helping friend of a patient's family. She was from a far country but had lived in the United States for several years. I knew she had some kind of job here, and she spoke with a distinct accent, revealing that she had not grown up with English as her mother tongue. After knowing this lady for several weeks, I was shocked to find out that she had studied and learned a couple of other languages totally unrelated to English or her own language. She had also earned two masters degrees in this country, and she had a very good job working for our local city.

It is so easy to quickly presume that we are better educated, wiser or more intelligent than others. I think we have also often met people who are indeed less educated than we might be, yet they somehow have a wisdom and intuition that far exceeds our own. Please do not let this intimidate you. If you are meek and humble, you can easily delight in getting to know people who know and understand more than you do. I am certainly well into the latter half of my own life here on earth, but my primary goal is still not to impress those around me. A primary goal of mine is still to listen and to learn.

After you have listened, when you have learned something about who a person is and where he is on his journey, you can then prayerfully meet him where he is, and point him to Jesus.

Great is the LORD, and greatly to be praised; And His greatness is unsearchable.

I will meditate on the glorious splendor of Your majesty, And on Your wondrous works.

The LORD is gracious and full of compassion, Slow to anger and great in mercy.

The LORD is good to all, And His tender mercies are over all His works.

The LORD upholds all who fall, And raises up all who are bowed down.

The LORD is righteous in all His ways, Gracious in all His works.

The LORD is near to all who call upon Him, To all who call upon Him in truth.

He will fulfill the desire of those who fear Him; He also will hear their cry and save them.

Psalm 145:3, 5, 8-9, 14, 17-19

III

DEPEND UPON GOD TO DO THE THINGS THAT ONLY GOD CAN DO.

God is at work among us. If He were not, we would just be spinning our wheels. It is God who has a matchless love for "your" patient. It is God who has a plan to work in the patient's life. It is God who knows what He is going to do here. We do well to get on board and ask God to graciously use us. God has the right to demand this of us, as we see in passages such as 1 Corinthians 6:19-20.

We also see that God wants us to willingly give complete control of ourselves to Him. A much treasured and hopefully well-known verse is Romans 12:1, where we read, "I beseech you, therefore, brethren, by the mercies of God, that you present your bodies a living sacrifice, holy, acceptable to God, which is your reasonable service." The Lord wants us to offer ourselves to be used as tools in His hands. That is a great picture.

The reality is that this is so easy to say and often so hard to do. When we remember to PRAY, we remind ourselves of Who is in charge, Who has the power, and Who gives the grace. I want to encourage you to pray, and then to pray some more. This is not a book on prayer, but I would like to remind you (and myself) again, that good things almost never happen without a lot of prayer and at least a little faith. There is a great story in the beginning of Acts 12. The clear truth is that the people involved here did a lot of praying, but apparently, they only had very little faith. God still answered. Check it out: *Acts 12:1-17.*

I would like to consider two roles that we sometimes try to assume for ourselves. But, these are roles that belong to God alone.

He is **Judge**. He is **Savior**. We are neither.

When we try to take on either one of these roles, we find ourselves fighting against the whole order of things that God has ordained. We soon frustrate ourselves and either confuse or offend those to whom we are trying to minister.

This should be an obvious truth, but we just might need one more gentle reminder. Only one sits as Judge over people. He is the second person of the Trinity, and His name is Jesus Christ. He is called, "Wonderful, Counselor, Mighty God, Everlasting Father, Prince of Peace." (Isaiah 9:6)

In John 5:21-23, Jesus Christ tells us some powerful truths. "For as the Father raises the dead and gives life to them, even so, the Son gives life to whom He will. For the Father judges no one, but has committed all judgment to the Son, that all should honor the Son just as they honor the Father. He who does not honor the Son does not honor the Father who sent Him."

This is a rather provocative passage for those who deny the deity of Jesus Christ.

So who is the only one who can ever rightfully judge you? Jesus Christ, the Lord. Jesus is also the only one who can ever rightfully judge your patient, or your spouse, your neighbor, your boss, or even your child.

We should try to be well informed. We should pray for discernment, but only one knows the whole story. Only one can look on the heart (I Samuel 16:7). Only one has the right to judge a human being. I often read Romans 8:31-39 to people I visit. In the light of what we just heard in John 5, please listen closely to Romans 8:34.

"Who is he who condemns? It is Christ who died, and furthermore is also raised, who is even at the right hand of God, who also makes intercession for us."

So, the only One who will ever judge me is the same One who died in my place to pay my sin's penalty. He is also the same One who is my defense attorney, interceding for me at the right hand of God the Father. This makes me endlessly thankful.

Matthew 7:1-2 is the classic passage warning us on this topic. "Judge not, that you be not judged. For with what judgment you judge, you will be judged, and with the measure that you use, it will be measured back to you."

Notice that in this same chapter of Matthew, verses 15-16 tell us to, "Beware of false prophets, who come to you in sheep's clothing, but inwardly they are ravenous wolves. You will know them by their fruits." Again in verse 20, "Therefore by their fruits you will know them."

I remember when I was just a young teenager and very new to the faith, hearing my pastor say, "You are not to judge, but it is important to be a good fruit inspector." The verses in Matthew 7 are clearly stated and, I think, not hard to understand. We should indeed pray for wisdom and discernment. We should be able to recognize teaching that is clearly false or hypocritical.

I think we all know that we need to study and be able to rightly divide the word of truth (2 Timothy 2:15). We also need to realize that dedicated Christian men and women, reading the same Scriptures, will sometimes come to different understandings of many details of doctrine and practice. This simply does not get me stirred up anymore. Honest, believing students of the Bible usually agree on the majority of their conclusions. The problem tends to be that many spend most of their time angrily disputing the relatively small number of topics on which they do not agree.

Church history gives us stories of battles, even bloody battles, fought over things that almost no one today seems to think are important. I would encourage you to seriously decide which clear truths are really important enough to earnestly defend or even to separate over. Then firmly stand upon the essential doctrines of the authority of the Bible, our Lord Jesus Christ, and His saving grace. And don't sweat the small stuff. The reality is that we are all fallen human beings. The tendency to judge others comes naturally for most of us.

So now it's time for a little confession on my part. I used to have judgmental thoughts toward others; those who followed God's call into the ministry, and later left the ministry. Then I found myself, at age 39, back in school and working full-time in a completely secular occupation.

I used to judge other parents when I saw the trouble their children got into. Then my own son started using alcohol and drugs and I found myself powerless to pull him out. I have gained a gut-level understanding of Matthew 7:1, "Judge not, that you be not judged."

Please take a few minutes to read Romans 14:1-4, and verses 10-13. I think both the message and the current applications should be clear.

The other role that only God can fulfill is **that of Savior.** We are called to be witnesses, telling others what we have seen and experienced. Like John the Baptist, you get to proclaim, "Behold! The Lamb of God, who takes away the sin of the world." (John 1:29) We have the opportunity to be like Andrew, who brought his brother, Simon Peter, to Jesus. When Philip spoke to Nathanael about Jesus and Nathanael mocked the very thought of how anything good could come out of Nazareth, Philip simply said, "Come and see." (John 1:40-50) Andrew and Philip never saved anyone by their own power, and neither did Nathanael or Peter, but they each shared what they had seen and heard and then God did the saving work. Now, as a result, there are hundreds of millions across the globe who claim the name of Jesus Christ as Lord. (1 John 1:1-5)

I believe God wants us, as His children, to be faithful in loving our neighbors and sharing the good news of the Gospel with them. The sick and dying are included in those who are our neighbors. When an expert in the law tried to get Jesus to narrow down his definition of "my neighbor,"

Jesus told us all the story of the Good Samaritan, found in Luke 10:25-37. The man who got help was one of the sick and dying. If you or I had come up with this story, we probably would have made the injured man be the Samaritan, and told the narrow-minded, cold religious crowd to help those outside their own circle.

What Jesus did was divine genius (of course). Jesus made the despised outsider be, not the victim, but the hero of His story. Then Jesus turned the lawyer's question completely right side up in verse 36. The lawyer had wanted to know who qualified as his neighbor. Jesus made it clear that our responsibility is to actually be the neighbor to all those we see around us. If we are willing to love and help anyone who is in need, even those who despise us, then I believe God can use us as His hero, no matter where we are or where we have come from.

Each of us can be honest, secure and realistic about who we are. We can allow the patient to be who he really is and we can try to meet him where he is. Then we can prayerfully follow Jesus as our all-powerful Savior and Lord. But even if we were to do all these things just right, there is still no guarantee that we will see the results that we might hope for. That's okay; God wants to use you as His faithful servant. God alone gets to choose whether He will use you as a Jeremiah or as a Jonah. No one turned when they heard Jeremiah. A huge city repented at the preaching of Jonah. God asks for faithfulness, and He gives the final outcomes. *By the way, which of these prophets seems to be held in higher esteem?*

You shall not take vengeance, nor bear any grudge against the children of your people, but you shall love your neighbor as yourself: I am the LORD.

You shall rise before the gray headed and honor the presence of an old man, and fear your God: I am the LORD.

And if a stranger dwells with you in your land, you shall not mistreat him.

The stranger who dwells among you shall be to you as one born among you, and you shall love him as yourself; for you were strangers in the land of Egypt: I am the LORD your God.

Leviticus 19:18, 32-34

IV

FOUR ESSENTIALS TO DO

The following are four ***action verbs***, telling us how we can be effective ministers to our patients. The first two are the most basic, but each of the four builds one upon the other. The last command rises above all else. When it comes down to it, none of the four should be taken and pursued independently from the others.

What should I do as I reach out to people in need?

RESPECT everyone

Respect is a significant and powerful thing. It seems to be one of the most basic needs of each individual. I confess that I have sometimes been annoyed when some people want to demand respect from others. Many of us have a tendency to want to see everyone earning the respect of others. Well, experience and the Bible have made me see that it is very important for me to simply give respect to each person I meet.

1 Peter 2:17 says "Honor all people. Love the brotherhood. Fear God. Honor the king." The word honor, also translated respect in some translations, is used here first to tell us how to approach every person we meet. Then the same word is used to tell us how to approach a king. Enough said.

Often we tend to respect a person for what they have achieved or for the position they hold in society. I now think we should respect people, just because God has given them the breath of life. In spite of all of our imperfections and problems, each human person is still, in some way, a reflection of God's own image. (Genesis 1:26)

It is amazing just how effective it can be to simply show respect to people. Sadly, it seems like respect tends to be generally given less today than it was a few decades ago. Respect is an important place to begin with every person we meet. This is especially true with people whose illness and or weakness has put them in a place where they have new limitations and needs. Many times, people who are ill will feel as if they have lost much of the respect they used to have from others. We can demonstrate that we care by showing respect with our words and our actions. Respect is naturally demonstrated by polite words and acts of kindness.

When we visit people in healthcare facilities and in their own homes, we encounter interesting opportunities to serve people in various ways. Jesus clearly served others in a great variety of ways. He even took on the lowly task of washing the feet of the Apostles. When you launch out to help those in need, you will likely have many opportunities to serve in various simple tasks. I can recall changing light bulbs and air filters, repairing equipment, moving furniture and even doing some pest control.

Showing respect for the people we meet also helps keep us in a proper place of healthy humility. So don't be surprised if you are given an opportunity to do occasional tasks that are "below your pay grade." Some wise person said that being humble is not so much about thinking less of ourselves, as it is about thinking of ourselves less. A great way to spend less time thinking of ourselves is to focus our attention and our respect on each one we are trying to help.

When older people begin to lose their mental abilities, they are still worthy of our respect. We learn to speak in simple words to people who have dementia. It is really not appropriate to talk down to any adult. We should not speak to an Alzheimer's patient as one might speak to a baby or a toddler. We do well to ask simple questions and allow plenty of time to for answers if our patient is able to answer at all. If she cannot answer, we can still respectfully affirm her for what she has done, and who she still is.

Affirmation is a great part of showing respect. If we look around a person's room and listen to what they and their family members have to say, we will almost always find something to affirm. This is a good practice that I wish I had learned much earlier in my life. Anyone can come up with a critical comment, but such words rarely reveal anything new and are almost never helpful or appropriate when ministering to the sick or the dying. A word of affirmation given with sincerity is like a cup of cold water in the desert or a perfect cup of coffee on a winter morning. Honest affirmation is a simple way to show respect and provide encouragement.

We also need to show respect to younger people. So often we can complain about how hard it is to communicate with younger people. Showing respect to them before expecting respect from them can help communication to begin. Can you remember starting high school as a freshman among bigger juniors and seniors, who sometimes mocked and looked down on you? Can you imagine now what it would have been like to have a senior respectfully befriend you without trying to take advantage of you? To the younger people you meet, you can be the older one who respectfully gives help and offers a sense of security as well.

In Paul's first letter to Timothy, he told this younger pastor, "Do not rebuke an older man, but exhort him as a father, younger men as brothers, older women as mothers, younger women as sisters, with all purity." 1 Timothy 5:1-2. The Greek verb translated, "exhort" is *parakaleo*, which literally means: to call alongside. This word can be used in many ways, but in this verse, it seems to include the idea of helping or encouraging. Those of us who have gotten a little older ourselves, might take this principle one generational step further and respectfully treat younger men and women just as we would want others to treat our own sons and daughters.

Sometimes, in order to understand what a principle means, it helps to consider what it does not mean. In order to respect, we should always avoid judging, especially on first appearances. It should be clear that pre-judging is never fair. The word prejudice is exactly this, the act of pre-judging. If I think I can determine who a person is by the color of his skin or the accent in his voice or his country of origin; then I am guilty of prejudice. I am hoping that no one reading this wants to act with prejudice, but I am afraid that each of us can tend to do so in subtle, yet harmful ways. A little awareness and honest self-examination can go a long way here.

Now let's consider the possibility of judging once we have, "acquired a lot of clear evidence." Please consider this. To rightfully judge someone, we would have to know all of the facts concerning this person, but we never do know all of the facts. Even if we could know all of the facts, we could never fully understand those facts or the experiences that someone else has been through. Part of my belief system is that there is One, who does have all of the facts and understanding. I am not Him, and never will be.

For about three years I had the opportunity to be active in a prison ministry, visiting people who were incarcerated for various crimes. I will mention here that I am respectfully thankful for those who enforce the law, and for those who serve us by working in prisons and penitentiaries. After getting to know a lot of people kept behind bars, I have often said to myself, "But for the grace of God, there go I." To respect someone does not mean we need to agree with him, and it certainly does not mean that we excuse every kind of behavior. I suppose there are some people who need someone to remind them of what they have done wrong, but practically everyone needs someone to show them that we still care about them as a person.

It is very important that we respect a person's emotional state as he or she goes through the grief of an illness or a major loss. We often encourage people who are grieving not to make any big or important decisions for as much as a year after the death of a loved one. Unfortunately, people face some decisions at such times that just cannot be delayed. It would be worse than disrespectful to try to persuade a grieving person to make any kind of financial decision that could benefit you or your organization. Putting on a "hard sell" even toward some noble spiritual decision might seem advantages, but pushing weakened people can have devastating consequences. People eventually know when they have been taken advantage of. People need kindness and respect.

Now comes a most important point. We should never tell someone how they should feel. It is all too easy to slip into this when we are just trying to give comfort. A patient gets a diagnosis of stage two colon cancer. One could quickly want to say, "You should be thankful that they found it before it had already become stage three or four." I don't know if you have ever had a physician tell you that you have cancer of any stage, but the normal reaction is a state of shock and dismay. It can take as long as a few weeks for a patient and his family to actually process what a cancer diagnosis means to them.

The patient's physician will normally be the one to tell the patient: the diagnosis, the treatment options and, many times, the odds of recovery. All of that is the doctor's job, not mine and not yours. We might do well to ask our friend how this news makes her feel but then listen to her feelings without critique. Feelings are often not reasonable at all. It almost always helps if a person can share his or her feelings with a calm, non-judgmental, compassionate listener. We cannot chase away someone's difficult or unpleasant feelings with logical arguments. We can give them an opportunity to put their feelings into words, which is an important step in making sense of it all.

I can recall being a new chaplain intern in a hospital, trying to convince patients not to be afraid. There was one patient in particular, in the ICU, who had a fear that was completely illogical. I could, oh so clearly, see how unreasonable her fear was, and I was so sure that I had the most bulletproof argument that would completely take away that fear. I presented my case, and I not only failed to vanquish her fear; I also offended her and pretty much demolished any trust and rapport that we had.

Just to serve as bad examples, here are a few ***very ill-advised*** and hurtful ***statements*** that I have personally heard a well-meaning person tell someone, regarding how they should feel after suffering a great loss:

- You should ***be glad*** you're still young.
- ***Be thankful*** that you have other children.

- ***Be glad*** they took your left arm since you are right-handed.
- It's been a whole year now. ***You should be over your grief by now***.

Again, please ***do not*** say such things. Do not try to tell people how they should feel. Instead, give them a safe place and an opportunity to share their emotions, knowing they will not be judged by you. Now, this is fortunately rare, but if the one you are trying to help tells you that he or she wants to hurt himself or someone else, please get some more help right away. Especially if this person has a plan of how to harm himself or herself, you need to tell their physician, chaplain or social worker. It can be good to know the number of a suicide hotline to pass along to your friend. Doing nothing is sometimes making a dangerous choice.

As we show respect for others we should naturally tend to want to listen to them. We have already mentioned some about listening, but now we want to dive into this essential topic more fully.

> **So then my beloved brethren,**
> **let every man be swift to hear, slow to speak, slow to**
> **wrath,**
> **for the wrath of man does not produce the righteousness**
> **of God.**
> **James 1:19-20**

LISTEN intentionally

It is hard to think of any task we do in ministering to people that does not in some way require good listening. Listening is a noble and gracious art that we all should strive to do better.

You cannot know what a person is thinking unless she tells you. She will not tell you what she is thinking unless you listen. You do not know what is going on in her life unless she tells you. She will not tell you unless you listen.

Here are some ***underlying principles*** that can help us to listen better. Later we will cover some practical steps.

Be Curious

Can you remember having a fascination with hearing, seeing and learning new things; of meeting new people, of hearing their stories? Remember the joy of eavesdropping? Common appearing people all around us are full of amazing stories and experiences. I have listened to thousands of life stories, and every one of them has been in some way interesting to me. Here are just a few extraordinary examples:

- I listened to the story of one of my patients who was with her parents when Bonnie and Clyde stole their car at gunpoint.
- I listened to a lady who ran into Clark Gable when he was a pilot in WWII.
- I met a man who, when he was a very little boy, shook hands with Adolf Hitler.
- I listened to at least three different men who stormed the beaches of Normandy.
- I listened to two or three different ladies who were the real, "Rosie the Riveter."

I have never met a truly famous patient, but I have never heard a life story that was boring either. A big part of being young at heart is being curious. A big part of being a good listener is that same curiosity. So next time you ride a bus or sit in a restaurant, go ahead and listen in on that nearby conversation. I won't tell.

Be Humble

Why is it better to be humble? Humble people are better listeners.

It is good to remember that everyone we meet knows some things that we do not know. Each one has seen things that we will never be able to see, and they understand some things that we do not yet understand. Most older people have gone through economic hardships and conflicts that we have only read about in history books. I love to listen to amazing stories told by eyewitnesses to history. The people we meet have done and endured things that are profound and important. Some have invented, developed or built things that have changed our lives. Tom Brokaw spoke of these as, "the greatest generation." I cherish the opportunity to stop and listen to these men and women. I want to learn from their experiences.

I remember listening for an hour with my mouth shut while an African American man clearly, and with great emotion, told me what it was like growing up in the South in the thirties and then fighting for his country in WWII, only to return from Europe and be treated as less than a man in the country for which he had risked his life. This is how we learn things that we really need to learn. Please listen with quiet humility.

Why is it better to be humble? James 4:6 tells us, "God resists the proud, But gives grace to the humble." 1 Peter 5:5 repeats the exact same words. I am sure that I want to receive all of His grace that I can.

Humility helps us understand that we still have a lot to learn. I am convinced that, if I am humble I will listen better. I also believe that, if I am humble the one I listen to will be more likely to share his or her thoughts and feelings with me.

Be Compassionate

In order to be the best kind of listener that we can be, it helps to have a healthy dose of compassion. The Apostle Paul and Jesus Himself give us, clear examples of what compassion can look like. Paul wrote in 1 Thessalonians 2:7-8, "But we were gentle among you, just as a nursing mother cherishes her own children. So, affectionately longing for you, we were well pleased to impart to you not only the Gospel of God but also our own lives, because you had become dear to us." I have to ask myself, do I really show that kind of compassion to those that I minister to? Hear also the words in John 11:33-36 from and about Jesus.

"Therefore, when Jesus saw her weeping, and the Jews who came with her weeping, He groaned in the spirit and was troubled. And He said, "Where have you laid him? They said to Him, Lord, come and see. Jesus wept. Then the Jews said, "See how He loved him!"

Compassion is not so much a thing of the head, to be studied and learned. Compassion belongs to the heart. If you have little compassion for people, something is seriously lacking. Some follow the pattern of our society too much. We are often taught that men should not show much compassion. I can remember many of the classic Westerns with men like John Wayne, Clint Eastwood, and Lee Van Clef. I dated a girl in high school whose Dad looked just like Lee Van Clef. Scary for me! Often in movies today, it's not just leading men, but "powerful" women are also portrayed as having little or no compassion.

Perhaps your own parents showed little compassion toward you. This can be a big factor in how we relate to others. In order to listen better, I hope you are asking,

"How can I be more compassionate?" Here are a few possible answers:

a. ***Remember*** what life has already taught you through your own experiences.
The difficulties we live through tend to teach us much more than books ever could. If you can recall the lessons learned in your own painful memories, they can greatly help you to have compassion for others.

Just to serve as examples, here is a list of some of my most memorable ordeals:

- I remember lying in bed with nausea; I could not even stand the smell of food.
- I remember having "frozen shoulder" and months of therapy that felt like torture.
- I remember sleepless nights with pain from broken ribs and an injured hip.
- I remember having to resign and leave a position that meant my life to me.
- I remember a Sunday morning in August, the day our only son died.

If we live very long at all, each of us will go through illness, pain and deep personal loss. These things are very hard, but they give us at least some idea of what those we minister to are going through. Remember, however, that the experiences of others are never exactly the same as your own experiences. So, **never say**, "Oh, I know how you feel."

b. **Imagine** what your patient is going through.
You may not find this helpful, but if you have a good imagination, it may actually be very effective. I do not have a great imagination but this still helps me to some extent.

c. **Ask God to help you** have compassion for those you minister to. God has reached out to us with great compassion, and He clearly wants us to show compassion to others. I find great confidence in asking God for something that He clearly wants me to have, and to share with others.

Now some very practical points about listening:

If you are talking, you are not really listening. If you are thinking about what you want to say, you are probably not listening.

Look at the one you are listening to. Let him see your whole face as you listen. A little boy told his father, who was reading the newspaper, "Daddy, listen to me with your eyes." You might also need to work on making more frequent eye contact, but don't be too intense with that either.

When I am visiting someone who is lying in bed, I always hunt down a chair to sit in. It is really not good to stand by someone in bed. Such an arrangement is not good for at least two reasons. First of all you are standing over the patient looking down on them. Secondly, standing there tends to convey the message that you are in a hurry. People are much more likely to feel at ease and open up in conversation if you are in a seated position. It is also good to be sure your body is turned toward the patient. It is good to lean a little forward toward the patient and avoid leaning back in an over relaxed position.

Try to avoid questions that can be answered by a yes or a no. Here are a couple examples: "Are you having a rough day today?" "It's no fun being here in the hospital is it?" Most of the time, we already know the answer to the yes/no questions that we might ask. It is far better to present a leading question that will encourage your patient to share his thoughts or emotions. You could form your own mental list or even write some ideas down. Just to serve as examples, here are some good leading questions to ask:

- "Could you tell me how you are feeling now?"
- "What has happened since I saw you last."
- "Tell me more about what you have been going through."
- "What was that like for you?"
- "Can you tell more about what this means to you?"
- "Wow! Could you tell me how that made you feel?"

I don't have these memorized, and you should not either. Just remember, you are inviting someone to share his thoughts, his experiences, and his feelings. You are not giving a test, but if you were, it would be an essay test, not true or false, and not multiple choice.

I used to think that a conversation had to be like playing tennis or volleyball. Both of those sports require an instant return of the ball. Your *conversation should be like* standing in the backyard with your son or daughter, just playing catch with all the time in the world. When the ball comes to you, you can simply hold it for a while. You don't need to have an instant response to everything that comes at you. Actually, it is good to *allow long pauses*. Some of the best things are said by a person after a long pause. The one you are visiting is thinking about how to word what he wants to say. Often he is mustering up the courage to say what he really wants to say. So learn to *be comfortable with periods of silence*. This is far more important than you might imagine. Also, do not be quick to introduce a new topic or question. Be sure your friend has finished with the current topic.

We can all work on becoming better listeners. I cannot think of a more needed, attainable human skill for ministering to others. There is hardly any aspect of human relationships that could not be improved by good listening.

> **Let no corrupt word proceed out of your mouth, but what is good for necessary edification, that it may impart grace to the hearers.**
>
> **And do not grieve the Holy Spirit of God, by whom you were sealed for the day of redemption.**
>
> **Let all bitterness, wrath, anger, clamor, and evil speaking be put away from you, with all malice.**
>
> **And be kind to one another, tenderhearted, forgiving one another, even as God in Christ forgave you.**
>
> **Therefore be imitators of God as dear children.**
>
> **And walk in love, as Christ also has loved us and given Himself for us, an offering and a sacrifice to God for a sweet-smelling aroma.**
>
> **Ephesians 4:29 – 5:2**

JOURNEY WITH

In Matthew 5:41 we find the words of Jesus, "…and whoever compels you to go one mile, go with him two." Jesus was telling His audience to go the extra mile with a Roman occupation soldier, who had the legal right to require any one of them to carry his pack for one mile. During the first mandatory mile, they had, and we have, the opportunity to respect and listen. During the second mile, I see the opportunity to journey with.

I was on call in the local hospital on a weekday when a young man was brought to the ER by ambulance. He had been driving a forklift in a nearby warehouse. The forklift somehow tipped over and crushed his foot. This horrible injury required the specialized skill of a foot surgeon. The surgeon was called and the patient was given strong pain medicine, but he could not be sedated before the specialist arrived to carry out what would be a very long surgery. The patient was still in terrible pain, and he had to wait for over an hour before anything else could be done. None of the medical staff in the ER could help him any further. My part was to simply sit with this suffering man. I stayed there with him, holding his hand and saying very little, for what seemed to me like a very long time. It must have seemed like an eternity to him. At that time I had a problem that I had to deal with. It was overwhelmingly difficult for me to be present with someone in pain. Up until then, I had always wanted to go run and get someone, anyone, who could make a patient's pain go away. I knew that no one could do that in this situation. No one else in the ER that day could do what I needed to do. The patient got through it somehow, and I was able to be present with his pain. That day I learned much about what it means to journey with.

Journeying with usually requires time and sometimes it requires sacrifice. Early in Ezekiel's life, as the Lord was preparing him for his prophetic ministry, we find an interesting verse. Ezekiel 3:15 reads as follows, "Then I came to the captives at Tel Abib, who dwelt by the River Chebar; and *I sat where they sat*, and remained there astonished among them seven days." In ministering to the sick, the dying and the grieving, you will likely learn what it means to "sit where they sit." Sometimes you too will be astonished. This might mean a long period of waiting in the ER or the ICU. It can mean spending many hours with a dying person and his family. It means becoming one with people you have seen as "others." *It might mean not seeing these as "them."*

I believe it is very important to be able to meet people where they are. We will have few opportunities to help if we expect people to first become what we want them to be before we reach out to them. Paul wrote in 1Corinthians 9 of making himself, "a servant to all, that I might win the more." A couple verses later, he wrote, "to the weak I became as weak, that

I might win the weak. I have become all things to all men that I might by all means save some." (I Corinthians 9:19 & 22)

I am rather adamant about being honest with people. Notice that Paul did not say that he pretended to be all things to all, but rather, "I have become all things to all men." I want to be willing to set aside my own personal opinions and preferences on the many meaningless things in life on this earth. When I first meet a family who has lots of banners on their walls for the University of Alabama, I probably won't tell them that I actually prefer Auburn. When I meet people from New England, I will probably tell them that my wife and I lived almost four years near Boston. I may or may not tell them how much more I prefer to live where we are now. It can be a positive thing to make note of common experiences. When I visit with a man who works as an auto mechanic, I may tell him that I enjoy working on my own cars, but I am quick to point out that I leave the difficult jobs to professionals like him. Please do not try to pretend you are someone that you are not. Think about this. If you go to a Harley Davidson convention, don't wear black leather pants unless you actually own a Hog.

Here is another important point. Perhaps you have noticed that we each seem to be given our own special difficulties in life? These are called such things as, "trials" or "challenges" or "chronic illnesses." The Apostle Paul had one of these, but no one knows for sure what it was. He called it his, "thorn in the flesh." Most of us have at least one of these ourselves. My most noteworthy "problem" is insulin-dependent diabetes that I have lived with for well over 40 years. I don't like my illness any more than you like yours, but each of our own particular challenges can actually give us an "unfair advantage." You see, when Paul complained about his problem, God told him,

"My grace is sufficient for you, for my strength is made perfect in weakness."
2 Corinthians 12:9

When I first read those words as a teenaged boy, it did a lot to change my outlook on my biggest apparent problem. I certainly did not want to be weak, but my unwelcome hindrance has taught me to lean more on God's strength. Each of our problems can also open doors to relate to and communicate with others who have similar challenges. When I meet someone suffering from the effects of diabetes, I often look him in the eye and say, "Guess what. I have had to struggle with this for a long time too." And, when I begin to feel the pain of arthritis in my hands, I gain a whole different level of understanding and compassion for others who suffer terribly with that horrible problem.

I believe it is important for each of us to pause and consider our own humanity and mortality. Unless you tragically die a sudden death, you will grow old. Your body will weaken and break down in one way or another. If you are still young, believe me; this happens faster than you could imagine. Youth and good health are wonderful things that this world treasures. Sadly these never last as long as we wish they would.

Working with dying people has brought me away from the rather common place of avoiding the idea of my own death, to a place of more peacefully accepting that it will happen one day. It is a good, mentally healthy thing to be able to reflect on one's own mortality. Most people would just rather not talk about death. Death is often the proverbial elephant in the room that no one wants to mention.

You have probably heard someone tell you that they are not afraid to die, it's just the process or the experience of dying that worries them. I have witnessed a few very difficult deaths, but most of the deaths that I have attended have been peaceful. Good palliative (comfort) care in the final weeks and hours of life makes a huge difference.

Doctors and nurses trained in end of life care can do much to minimize a patient's pain, and also to control other possible issues such as nausea and terminal restlessness. Social workers and volunteers can be available to give support. I see part of my role as a chaplain to gently help the patient to come to a place of assurance that he is at peace with God, at peace with his family and friends, and even at peace with himself.

Many times patients and family members want to know when death will come. Sometimes we think we have a pretty good idea of when a person will die, but experience shows that we can only rarely predict the time of death with much accuracy. We are often surprised by a death that comes more quickly than we expect, and we are also frequently amazed by how long some people are able to hold onto life. I have observed that the people who are most likely to amaze us with their endurance are "the ladies in their eighties." When a patient is declining towards death, I often report in my visit notes, "Helped family to reflect on the unknown timing of coming death of this patient." I have come to accept that it actually is good that we do not know precisely when death will come.

Many people have told me that they would prefer to die suddenly in their sleep one night. The problem with such an exit strategy is that such a death gives no one the chance to say their final goodbyes, nor does it give the dying one that last opportunity to find peace.

> **Therefore, as the elect of God, holy and beloved, put on tender mercies, kindness, humility, meekness, longsuffering;**
>
> **bearing with one another, and forgiving one another, if anyone has a complaint against another; even as Christ forgave you, so you also must do.**
>
> **But above all these things put on love, which is the bond of perfection.**
>
> **And let the peace of God rule in your hearts, to which also you were called in one body; and be thankful.**
>
> **Let the word of Christ dwell in you richly in all wisdom, teaching and admonishing one another in psalms and hymns and spiritual songs, singing with grace in your hearts to the Lord.**

And whatever you do in word or deed, do all in the name of the Lord Jesus, giving thanks to God the Father through Him.

Colossians 3:12-17

Choose to LOVE

These first three essentials have gone from most basic and foundational to more active and involving. Again, none of the four principles named here are sufficient to stand alone. They tend to build upon one another, and this last one is the noblest of all.

I think we all love Love. Perhaps every individual has their own way of understanding what this wonderful concept is. Our modern English usage of the word takes in so many different things. Probably for most of us, the first thought that comes to mind is the idea of romance. Most adults in America do get married, and hopefully, that has a lot to do with romantic love.

In another direction, we have all made casual comments about how we just "love" some favorite food or automobile or style of music. The point is, if we are to consider loving people who are sick or dying, we should think about what we mean by this word.

The love that I want to propose here is the *agape* love found in the New Testament. There are a couple of other Greek words that also get translated as "love" in English translations of the Bible, but I will just stay with verses that use the word *agape* here.

The first letter of St. Paul to the Corinthians has a magnificent and well-known chapter that is dedicated to this word. I am about to give you a few of the verses here, but I would recommend that you look in your own Bible and read all of 1 Corinthians 13. The first verses tell us how none of our abilities, talents or good deeds count for anything if we do not love. Then we come to the following definition found in verses 4 through 8:

"Love is patient, love is kind and is not jealous; love does not brag and is not arrogant, does not act unbecomingly; it does not seek its own, is not provoked, does not take into account a wrong suffered, does not rejoice in unrighteousness, but rejoices with the truth; bears all things, believes all things, hopes all things, endures all things. Love never fails;"

The verses that follow these remind us that so many of the things we might value here end up being short-lived. Then comes the final verse, "And now abide faith, hope, love, these three; but the greatest of these is love." I firmly believe that love is the greatest motivating force that God gives to us. A sense of duty or even a sense of guilt can motivate us for a while, but when it comes to keeping us going, and giving and sacrificing over the long road of life, nothing motivates like love.

It is remarkable to me how many times in the Bible we are "commanded" to love. Jesus clearly embraced the earlier commands to love, found in the Hebrew Scriptures. In Matthew 22, beginning in verse 35 (and also in Mark 12) a teacher of the Law said to Jesus, "Teacher, which is the great commandment in the law?" Jesus responded, **"You shall love the Lord your God with all your heart, and with all your soul, and with all your mind."** This was a quote of Deuteronomy 6:5. Then Jesus went on a bit. "This is the great and foremost commandment. The second is like it, **You shall love your neighbor as yourself."** This second quote was from Leviticus 19:18.

It becomes obvious that love must be more than just a feeling that might come over us. Love is a command. Actually, love is the obeying of a command. As obvious as this sounds, it also sounds a little radical.

So love is a choice to be made with all of the "heart, soul and mind." In Matthew 5:44 Jesus challenged us to choose to do something that is extremely difficult. He said. "But I say to you, love your enemies and pray for those who persecute you." In Romans 12, the apostle Paul repeated much of what Jesus taught about choosing to love those who are the most difficult to love. The last verse of Romans 12 reads, "Do not be overcome by evil, but overcome evil with good." In Paul's letter to the Ephesians, we read, "Be kind to one another, tender-hearted, forgiving each other, just as God in Christ also has forgiven you. Therefore be imitators of God, as beloved children; and **walk in love, just as Christ also loved you** and gave Himself up for us, an offering and a sacrifice to God as a fragrant aroma." Ephesians 4:32 – 5:2

I know that even when we hear these wonderful words, we cannot fully grasp the meaning of this love. Perhaps the essential key is to first be personally embraced by God's love yourself. Then the goal becomes an extending of this freely given love to others. Perhaps the best we can ever do is to become something like a pipeline sending love on down the way. 1John 4 is another great love chapter. You might want to read 1 John 4:7-21. John writes so simply and directly. Verse 11 says to us, "Beloved, If God so loved us, we also ought to love one another."

I want to mention here that as a chaplain, I have been taught more than once about maintaining "boundaries" with my patients. I do appreciate the importance of this. People who don't maintain some kind of emotional boundaries do not usually stay in this kind of ministry very long. The danger is that we can begin to see each of our dying patients as we would our own parent or spouse or sibling. An excess of grief and loss can turn into "burnout."

There is a downside to getting too close, but there is also a serious downside to never getting close at all. We work with people who are loved by God. These are our neighbors. God told us to love our neighbors. I tend to think that dying neighbors usually need even more love than healthy neighbors.

I am convinced that God is quite eager to help us to love one another. Many would say that the greatest example of human love is found in the love of a mother for her child. And why should the love of a father be any less? God seems to give such love so naturally that we have come to just expect it, and we are shocked when it appears to be absent. Our love for those around us, especially those who are suffering or grieving, should be just as natural. Parents who adopt a child make a choice to take in and care for a little one as their own. Not always, but most of the time, once the decision is made and the steps are taken in the process of adoption, the love seems to flow from parent to child, and soon in the other direction as well.

Some of the greatest examples of love that I have observed have been the love of a family member for their dying loved one. I have so often seen a husband or a wife caring for their spouse and children caring for a parent with amazing grace and patience. I remember one occasion staying by the bedside of a dying man with his grieving wife. Eventually, she told me that she had already cared for and buried not one, but two previous husbands. I was overwhelmed trying to imagine such love and such loss. Again, I firmly believe that love is the greatest motivating force that can be given to us.

If you are wondering whether you can really love the people you encounter, here is what I would be so bold as to recommend. Pray, first of all, asking God to show you how much He loves you. Then recall the best examples of human love you have seen. Then pray some more, even before each visit you make. Ask God to give you a love for hurting people that can touch them, and make a difference in their lives.

When discussing respect at the beginning of these pages, I said it is something that people really need and long for. Love is something that we probably need and long for even more. Just as most people respond to expressions of respect, they also respond to expressions of this kind of love. Many today tend to be skeptical and often slow to believe that our respect or our love is genuine. We need to be patient with these, remembering what we read in I Corinthians 13, "Love is patient, love is kind … love endures all things. Love never fails."

Here are two true stories that hopefully will serve to illustrate in a personal way what love can mean, what love for a patient might look like.

I was asked to call upon a lady in her early seventies who had lung cancer. She gave her permission for chaplain visits, so I had the opportunity to come to her tiny house in a lower middle-class area. Betty was a bit skeptical about me on the first visit. Only later, after she had shared much of her life story, did I begin to understand why she might be dubious of any stranger coming to visit. I asked her how she felt physically. At that point, she had been told that her cancer was terminal, but she was not in much pain. She had some shortness of breath and had already lost a lot of weight. I asked about her family situation. She had a son, who sometimes stayed with her, and another son who lived in the same county, not too far away. Betty also had sisters, and with them came some nieces and nephews, but they lived in other states, too far away to allow for many visits.

Betty did not share anything about her late husband until after we had known each other for many months. When I asked about any church connections, Betty said that she had attended a nearby Church but the new pastor had not come to visit her. She said she missed the old pastor. I told Betty that I could contact her church, as I knew that it was almost certain that the pastor would respond to a request from a chaplain. That first visit with Betty was not very profound, but I did reach her pastor later that day, and he came out to visit once or twice. I was able to come on Wednesdays, every week or two.

I showed Betty that I was very willing to listen to whatever she wanted to share. She only shared a little for the first several weeks, but soon there was a trust being built. Betty began to tell sad stories about how her alcoholic husband had done what alcoholic husbands often do. She told of trying to protect her sons and herself from his drunken rages. I would listen and then almost always read a few Bible verses during our visit, and I always said a prayer. At the beginning, it was just the Lord's Prayer, but then I added freely spoken prayers from the heart. I would assure Betty, telling her, "You know, the Lord loves you." She would respond, "I sure hope He does." Betty had not really experienced as much love as one would hope for. When life and people hand us a lot of disappointments, it tends to be more difficult to believe that God really loves us. I had good opportunities to keep building trust and showing loving kindness to Betty. That is an old word, but it is my favorite word in the Psalms.

There was no one big, earthshaking event that I saw during my visits with Betty, but eventually, it became clear that she had come to understand that the Lord Jesus truly did love her, and she was able to personally trust Him. I looked forward to our visits probably as much as Betty did. I came to continue to encourage and affirm, and I suppose I even did a little teaching. We talked about the wonder of the grace and love that God has extended to us, and about the glorious eternity that He has prepared. I can, without a doubt, say that I came to love Betty. She became sort of like a favorite aunt to me. Betty's decline had been gradual, but then it was more rapid. She became extremely thin and then bedridden. The last few days, Betty was on continuous care, with a nurse in her home around the clock, and I came every day.

When Betty became nonresponsive, my ministry as a chaplain turned more to her sons, who were also more present by that time. I wish I had been at Betty's bedside at the time of her death, but I was only able to arrive soon afterward. I mourned her loss, I still miss her, and I look forward to sharing more visits with her in Heaven. My relationship with Betty is a nice example of hundreds of encounters with patients over the years. I can only wish that all of my relationships with my patients turned out as wonderful as this one did.

Now I want to share a very different story, one that happened in a hospital ER. This is a gripping example of love that unfolded in a different way, and an opportunity that lasted only hours, rather than months.

Late on a weekday evening, I was the chaplain on call at a local hospital. The loudspeaker rang out, "Code blue in the ER." As always, this made my adrenaline rush as I half jogged toward the emergency room. A patient had just arrived in an ambulance, and her family members were on their way in their own car. I stopped very briefly to glance into trauma room #1, just to get some idea of what the condition of our patient might be. She was a "full arrest." The EMT guys had "bagged her" and were doing CPR, which is never as calm and gentle as it looks on the television shows. Experience said that the odds were very strongly against this woman surviving. The medical pros were doing all they could, but the extremely pale color of the patient was not at all encouraging.

I went straight to the family room to wait for the patient's family to arrive. Soon two frantic women hurried into the room, escorted by one of the hospital employees. The first woman was the patient's daughter. She was probably about 50 years old. The other was her daughter (the patient's granddaughter), perhaps 20 years old. The granddaughter appeared very timid and would hardly speak a word during the entire episode. The middle-aged daughter quickly revealed her relationship to the patient as she exclaimed, "My mother just can't die! She can't!" I told the daughter and granddaughter that I was the hospital chaplain, and I would be here with them while we waited for a doctor to come and give us some kind of news.

As you might expect, I was already praying about this intense situation and was observing and listening to these fearful, grieving women. At that time, I had only been taking on-calls as a hospital chaplain for a few months, and I found myself feeling a little anxious. I looked at the ladies' jewelry, hoping to get some hint of their background because sometimes a necklace or a ring might at least show if a person is Catholic or Protestant. I hope I did not let my surprise show, but the jewelry that I saw on these women told me a very different story. They both wore lots of rings on their fingers and toes, showing dragons and other clear symbols of an occult direction.

I started praying even more. I silently, but earnestly, told the Lord that I did not know what to do here, and I needed His help. The answer came clearly; these women needed love and compassion just as any other family members would need in this situation. I found myself praying rather desperately that somehow the mother in the trauma room would survive. I was very concerned about how things would go with these ladies if the patient died.

It was probably only 15 to 20 minutes (a very long 15 to 20 minutes) after the daughter and granddaughter arrived that a male ER doctor and one of the female nurses knocked on the door and came into the family room. I knew instantly what the doctor would say. It was written on both of their faces, but the family members had to hear it. The doctor gave the standard statement, "I'm sorry Ma'am. We did all that we could, but we could not save your mother's life. She has died." As soon as these words were spoken, the daughter threw herself onto the floor, crying uncontrollably and screaming her denial of this terrible new reality. The doctor and nurse had to get back to helping other patients in the ER, so I got on my knees on the floor beside her with a hand on her shoulder, while the granddaughter stayed in her chair crying into her hands. This went on for some time, but this was not a time to hurry. This was not a time to say any insightful words. It was a time to meet these two in their place of grief and loss. It was a time to show compassion and love with very few words.

It took quite a while for the daughter to gain enough composure to say anything more than, "No, no, she can't be dead." The two ladies never did really say much to one another. The daughter seemed focused on her own intense, even raging grief. I told her, "I can see you are very upset. You love your mother very much, don't you?" (I usually do not use the past tense when talking to a grieving person about one who has just died.) Eventually, the daughter was able to get up off the floor. Eventually, she shared some of her feelings in words, but she remained more guarded than most people I had met in an ER family room. After 30 or 40 more minutes, I told these two women that we could probably go back to see the mother's body if they thought they might be ready to do so. I asked them if I could leave for just a few minutes to go back to the trauma room and see how everything looked. I actually told these women that I wanted to be able to describe to them what they were going to see.

The trauma room was empty except for the pale, cold body of the mother, which was covered to her neck by a plain white sheet. Her eyes were closed, which always seems to be better for the family members than to see open or half-open eyes that are lifeless and glazed over. Death is often a very harsh thing to see. The patient had been "bagged" before she arrived in the ER, but the large clear plastic tube that had been coming up out of her mouth had been removed. This told me that the medical examiner had already released her body in a telephone call with the ER doctor. Normally the body is actually examined by the medical examiner only if there are suspicions about the cause of death.

I spoke with one of the nurses near the main desk, just across from the trauma room, asking if it would be okay to bring the daughter and granddaughter back to see the patient now. She said, "Sure we've got her all cleaned up already." I got back to the family room and found the two women still sitting silently next to each other in their chairs. I described to them both, as best I could, what they would see; then we slowly walked together to the trauma room. I pulled back the curtain and led them into the large, white, tiled room, walls lined with equipment and supplies, and a trauma bed locked into place in the middle of the floor. The daughter walked haltingly ahead of the granddaughter, who held tightly to her arm. The daughter reached out to touch her mother's body, then suddenly threw herself across her mother's body and began crying out again. I placed a hand on her arm, as much to steady her as to offer her comfort. The granddaughter wept again also, standing on the other side of her own mother. It took several minutes before these two were ready to go back to the family room.

Now there was more to be done. I asked if they had ever made any funeral plans, or had any contacts with a funeral home that they might choose. As usual in such unexpected deaths, they had no idea whom they should call. I pulled out a copy of the yellow pages that we kept in the family room and turned to the funeral home section. I was careful not to recommend a funeral home but was able to go down the list, tell them something about locations and even which ones tended to be more expensive. Having the responsibility to make this decision helped the daughter to focus on something she could have some control over. This seemed helpful.

Once the call was made, it took almost an hour before the funeral directors arrived and "received the body." Before they got there, we waited and I encouraged the daughter and granddaughter to share what they could about the one who had died. There were more silent moments of waiting than there were words shared. Listening is not just hearing, often it is waiting, just hoping to hear something. In their grief, these two softened somewhat but remained guarded.

Then I remembered to ask a rather routine question, "Does your mother have any jewelry that..." The daughter gasped and fear showed on her face. "I have to take off her jewelry!" Then I remembered the kind of jewelry that the daughter and granddaughter wore. I realized that the daughter probably did not want the funeral directors to see the occult jewelry on her mother. I got a bottle of liquid hand soap to make the swollen fingers slippery, and we went back to the trauma room, where the daughter and granddaughter removed all of the mother's rings from her fingers and toes.

Soon after, the men from the funeral home came and took the body of this woman to their funeral home. It had been about two hours since I heard the code blue call. I had done a lot of praying during that time, but I did not pray out loud with these family members. I had not mentioned God or spoken the name of Jesus. At that moment, I seriously thought I had failed to do my part in ministering to them. We were beginning to say our goodbyes when, to my surprise, the daughter put her arms around me in a very emotional hug. I got a lot of hugs in the ER and the ICU, but I do not remember many that were more meaningful than that one. The daughter then looked me in the eyes and said, "You will never know how much you have done for us. Thank you, thank you so much." To which I simply replied, "Thank you, and God bless you."

As far as I know, I have never seen these two women again. I have prayed for them many times since, and still do when the Lord brings them to mind. I do not know what has happened to them since the day they came into the ER, but I am sure that I did my part as a Christian minister to love and to bless those who, earlier that day, might have counted themselves as my enemies.

We already referred to Matthew 5:44 where Jesus says, "But I say to you, love your enemies, bless those who curse you, do good to those who hate you, and pray for those who spitefully use you and persecute you."

We also already mentioned Romans 12:21 "Do not be overcome by evil, but overcome evil with good."

There is no need to compromise the wonderful truths upon which we stand. We are commanded to show the love and grace of God to all people. We should rejoice in every opportunity to speak the truth in love and demonstrate our love by acts of kindness.

But the wisdom that is from above is first pure, then peaceable, gentle, willing to yield, full of mercy and good fruits, without partiality and without hypocrisy.

Now the fruit of righteousness is sown in peace by those who make peace.

James 3:17-18

GUIDELINES TO FOLLOW

1. <u>Don't try to point to some kind of "silver lining"</u> or some "positive aspect" in a person's suffering or in their family member's death. This is actually very similar to the mistake of trying to tell a patient or family member how she should feel. We discussed this within the chapter called Essentials in the last part of the section on Respect. The examples that were given there also apply well here. Romans 12:15 tells us an extremely important principle: "Rejoice with those who rejoice and weep with those who weep."

So often, we jump in and want to "cheer up" those who weep. Such attempts are misguided and they really do not help. Trying to cheer up grieving people very often just encourages the weeping one to cover up his sadness, or shove it down to some dark place, where it really does not go away. I wish I was better at weeping with those who weep. Before becoming a chaplain, there actually were many years that went by without me shedding a tear. That is not healthy for a human being. In the past several years I have wept much more, but I still wish I had a softer heart to share with others.

When we do point to some "positive side," in a grief situation, we are actually *minimizing* what the grieving person is going through. If we do this, our words, at the very least, shout loudly that we just don't get what they are going through. Such positive "cheer up" words can also be deeply insulting to the one who is suffering. Again, the patient needs to tell others what she is going through, and if you minimize her situation, she generally will shut you out, hide her grief and/or feel insulted. Please, please allow people to grieve. Give them a safe place and a welcoming opportunity to pour out their God-given emotions. Grief and tears are not a sign of weak faith. They are a usually a sign of strong love.

In further clarification of this important guideline, I want to ask you to seriously consider the importance of not falling into the practice of saying thoughtless clichés to sick or grieving people.

The phrases listed here are found in Alan Wolfelt's book *Healing a Friend's Grieving Heart.*

Please do not say such things as:
"Give it time... Keep busy...Be strong...At least he didn't suffer...It's time to move on...He lived a long life...Try not to think about it...You'll become stronger because of this...Be glad you had him as long as you did...He wouldn't have wanted you to be sad...Life is for the living."[1]

It is best to avoid these religious clichés also:
"It was God's will... God only gives you what you can handle... Now she's in a better place... This is a blessing... Now you have an angel in heaven."[2] (Another one I have heard that really made me angry is this, "God needed your Daddy more than you did.")

Please feel free to say:
I'm sorry you are going through this, but I don't want you to feel like you are alone.

I am going to keep praying for you.

I love you and your family.

I want you to know, I loved (and/or admired) James. [3]

You have my phone number. I want you to call me and let me know how I can help you with any needs, even if you just need someone to listen to you.

Joan, you have taken such wonderful care of James.

He knew he was loved by you.

By the way, it is very good to say out loud the name of the one who has died. If the patient is still living, but non-verbal, it is still important to frequently speak his or her name.

It is also very good to affirm God's love and compassion for the hurting and the grieving. I do this, almost without exception, at every visit that I make. If the one you minister to reacts with anger when you tell him that God loves him and cares, please do not feel as though you have to defend God. You are clearly present with this hurting and angry person. Let him see your love and faith in a kind and gentle way. This grieving person's attitude might change quickly, or it might take a long time, but arguing for God is really not going to help. God routinely uses loving kindness and grace to touch hearts that are broken. In Jeremiah 31:3 we find Jeremiah quoting God as He says,

"Yes, I have loved you with an everlasting love: Therefore with lovingkindness I have drawn you."

2. Never say, "I understand," although it is very often good to eventually say, "I believe God understands what you are going through." Psalm 147:5 states, "Great is our Lord, and mighty in power; His understanding is infinite." In Psalm 31:7, David says to the Lord, "I will be glad and rejoice in your mercy, for you have considered my affliction, you have known my soul in adversity." The Lord does comprehend the depths of each soul, but please realize that you and I cannot really understand the grief of another person. I do not even claim to understand my own grief.

A comment that I have often heard usually goes something like this, "I know how you feel. My *brother, wife, or son* died last year." Although our experience may come close to that of someone else on the surface of things, please do not think that a similarly sad situation could possibly make you understand the heart of another. Also, please try very hard ***not to compare one grief to another.*** Comparisons actually seem to end up as judging, or at least in some way trying to measure or quantify that which cannot be measured. This usually ends up being hurtful to someone.

Let me tell another experience that drove this lesson home to me. Late one weekday morning in the ICU, I was doing my chaplain duty of shuffling back and forth between two different families, each of whom had a loved one in the ICU. I spent time with each family, listening empathetically as

I had been trained to do. Both of the patients were in critical condition, and neither one of them was expected to live very much longer. I guess I might have been feeling a little smug, or at least rather satisfied with the way that I was "meeting these people where they were."

Then something happened. A nurse from one of the surgery departments whom I recognized, but did not really know, said to me, "Aren't you Becky's dad?" "Yes," I answered, "Becky, who works in outpatient surgery." The nurse then said, "Oh, well; Becky cut her hand on a wheelchair while helping a patient to her car. They took her to the ER." My heart sank in my chest, and a sick feeling of grief and fear went right through me. I immediately told one of the ICU staff that I was going to see my daughter in the ER, and I began quickly making my way the 200 yards to the other end of the hospital. The report I heard was certainly nothing disastrous, but this was my little girl (19 years old at that time), and I needed to go to her, to see her, and help her somehow. Somewhere during that short, hurried journey to the ER, it hit me. I just got walloped by my own emotions. I realized that I had no idea of what these families in the ICU were going through. Once I got to my daughter, I saw that she was far less upset than I was. Her hand just needed a couple of stitches. She was not in any great pain and there would be no permanent damage. I was greatly relieved, but I learned an important lesson. I learned that I really did not understand what my patients and their families were going through.

Again, even if we have, at some time, gone through a situation that sounds very similar to what our patient is going through, we still cannot understand what that particular patient is feeling. Each one of us has a different background, different experiences, and our own unique personality.

3. Don't be in a hurry. Even if you feel pressed for time, it's probably best not to tell the patient that you are. Almost without exception, when I have told a patient that I am in a hurry, nothing productive happened in that visit. Sometimes we do have to keep a visit brief, but I have learned not to announce at the beginning of a visit that I needed to rush. Here is another point along the same line. It is really wise to allow time to think before we speak. You probably have often heard the words found in James 2:19,

"… let every man be swift to hear, slow to speak, slow to wrath." So if you must get in a hurry, be in a hurry to listen. Words that I have regretted later are usually words that I said quickly.

It really is a good idea to first silently say in your head what you think you want to say. Then *maybe* say it out loud. Many times, I have been very thankful that I did this. Other times I have wished that I had. This is especially important when you are just beginning in this field, and also when speaking with someone you don't know very well yet.

4. <u>Don't immediately try to shoot down your patient's belief system</u>. If your patient says that he follows some unusual new age ideas or some other non-Christian religion, you should still show respect by listening to his own account of what he believes.

For a few years, I was assigned by my employer to help with volunteer training. I was told to teach on religious and cultural diversity. Maybe they picked me for this because I had lived for several years in a different country with a different language. They asked me to teach some basics about various other religions that patients might be practicing. A lot could be said about this, but I really want to try to make one point clear. If you or I go to visit with a person who has been raised in some other world religion, and we tell him, "Oh, I know a lot about your religion", and then I proceed to give some juicy bits of information that I have read about his religious traditions, what have I accomplished? At best I will come across sounding childish, and at worst, I will badly insult this person. You and I have some idea about how complex and diverse the beliefs and practices of various Christian denominations are. There are also vast and extreme variations within Buddhism, Islam, and Hinduism, just to name three other big world religions. Even a university professor of world religion could easily get himself in a difficult situation by trying to tell someone else what he supposedly believes.

What I taught the volunteers I was entrusted with was this: knowing a little about the basic background and history of other religions might well be helpful. What I would do with that information is simply let it keep me, hopefully, from offending my neighbor. Then I would ask the person if he or she would like to share with me some of what the beliefs and practices of his religion are. Remember all that we said about listening in that section called Essentials? The patient or family member will likely appreciate you for listening to him. He will now be more likely to trust you, and maybe to eventually listen to what you have to share. The patient or family member will need to think about what he actually does believe. He will have to think about it in the face of a terminal condition. Remember, you are asking God to help you love this person, right? You will also find out something about what kind of a Buddhist or Muslim he is. You will almost certainly hear some of his personal history.

You will want to listen and also show respect even if you cannot agree with anything he believes. You might want to kindly ask him how his belief system has changed his life. In conversations with people of other religions or philosophies there is no need to attack or in any way to insult. Christianity is unique in its claims and promises. I never feel that I need to apologize for my Christian faith. With a humble spirit, we can each do our best to represent our risen Savior in whom we trust. If your patient has a story to tell of his experience in his religion, listen to his story. He might just ask you to share your story. Humility always belongs in our own salvation story. Compassion and love will win more points than any argument. Again, in our most difficult encounters we do well to remember Romans 12:9-21. Love, prayer and patience all belong here.

I would like to think that I do not even need to refer to this next story, but I will anyway. It involves a huge lack of understanding in two of our favorite Apostles. Luke 9:51-56 gives us a narrative about Jesus and His disciples on their way to Jerusalem.

"Now it came to pass, when the time had come for Him to be received up, that He steadfastly set His face to go to Jerusalem, and sent messengers before His face. And as they went, they entered a village of the Samaritans, to prepare for Him. But they did not receive Him, because His face was set for the journey to Jerusalem. And when His disciples James and John saw this, they said, "Lord, doYou want us to command fire to come down from heaven and consume them, just as Elijah did?" But He turned and rebuked them, and said, "You do not know what manner of spirit you are of. For the Son of Man did not come to destroy men's lives but to save them."

The pastor I worked under, when I was in my mid-twenties told me a story from his own experience when he too was an assistant pastor. Ken was fresh out of Bible College, full of knowledge and zeal. He was sent by his pastor to visit a family who, as it turned out, were influenced by a different denomination and held a different opinion on baptism and some other doctrines. Ken knew lots of verses on what he believed, so he zealously "went at it" with the couple. Ken came back to report to his pastor, declaring that he had been victorious, clearly winning the argument against these people. His pastor's only question was, "Well, do you suppose they will be coming to our services this Sunday?" I am sure you realize by now that if we focus on winning an argument, we are most likely going to lose the relationship and the opportunity to be of any real spiritual help. People need to be loved first and foremost.

5. Don't stomp on a patient's hope. (This goes for the patient's family as well.)

I frequently meet a patient or family member who is totally focused on the hope that the patient will be healed of his or her terminal illness. Well, isn't hope right there in 1 Corinthians 13:13, with faith and love on either side of it? Yes, hope is a wonderful, needed commodity. But here is the reality that I have seen over more than a dozen years of working with thousands of patients. I have seen two or three patients who, in the stated opinion of physicians, were miraculously healed.

One of these was a fairly young man who had abused his own body with drugs, and his godly mother prayed for him. The surgeons were going to amputate his gangrenous arm, but at the last moment decided not to, only because the infection had already spread well up into his shoulder. It was too late to stop the infection by amputating his arm. As I understood it, the patient's new prognosis was that he would die fairly soon.

I was in the ICU the day after the canceled surgery, when the surgeon came back to do a follow-up assessment of the patient's condition. The surgeon came out of the patient's room with a dazed look on his face, speaking of a miracle. This physician was not a religious man. He told the ICU nurses, and he told me, that the tissues in the patient's arm and shoulder that were dead yesterday were now living tissues.

Later that same week, I watched this patient sign his own discharge papers with the same hand and arm that were supposed to be amputated just a few days earlier. I hope this miracle did something to truly change the heart and life of this man, but I do not know what became of him.

One other miracle I witnessed involved the healing of a pastor's wife (I will call her Mary) who had numerous problems that culminated in a brain bleed and surgery. Multiple physicians, who treated her in the hospital, all agreed that Mary had no hope of recovery and would never be alert again, much less able to communicate. Her husband prayed with amazing determination. The deacons and other pastors of their church came together to Mary's bedside to pray. The doctors were amazed when Mary woke up, then eventually began to respond, and then to speak. Months later, I was there to see Mary walk up onto the platform in church, where she told her story of miraculous recovery to hundreds of people. I also have a great memory of a time when I was visiting another patient who happened to be a member of this same church. This marvelously recovered Mary and her husband knocked on the door. They had both come to visit my patient themselves. After all of this took place, Mary was able to actively continue to serve the Lord along with her husband for a few years. Then rather suddenly, with no time of illness, Mary died. She was in her seventies.

I shared these two stories just to give testimony that I have seen just a little bit of how powerful and capable God is. When He chooses, God can certainly deliver a human from disease and death, for as long as He wishes. But think about this, please. Even though Lazarus was actually raised from the dead, his mortal body did not go on living for another hundred years. He had to die again. Throughout the centuries, one generation after another has yielded up their spirits as their mortal bodies have died. I have ministered to probably a dozen or more patients who were over 100 years of age, but every one of them eventually died. Life here is always temporary.

Our hope clearly needs to be in God's eternal promises, first and foremost, not in what this temporary world has to offer for a little while. That is easily said.

Now for a personal story about hope that was very instructive to my heart. I was assigned to visit a patient who was about 40 years old. He had a diagnosis of a terminal cancer; we will call him Brian. This man was very expressive of his faith in Christ. He believed that the Lord was going to heal him, and then use him to bring about a great spiritual awakening in the lives of others. I had already watched other patients die from the same type of cancer that Brian had. Most of these others whom I had ministered to were also young, and some were also full of faith.

I knew I should **respect** Brian's conviction that he would be healed, and I knew that I should **listen** to his heart as he went through his battle with the disease. I had already learned not to argue against hope. I knew it was best to listen and just be there. I knew that the progression of the disease would eventually, in most cases, take away a patient's denial. I hoped that the reality of his declining condition would help Brian focus his hope on eternal promises rather than on a temporary healing of the body. But somehow all of this was harder for me when it came to Brian. He was well oriented and well spoken. He had a good knowledge of the Bible and he pushed me on what I believed would happen to him. Somehow, out of respect and admiration for the great faith that Brian demonstrated, I ended up discussing with him, at length, the issue of expecting healing versus accepting the terminal diagnosis.

I shared my own belief that God can, and occasionally does, miraculously heal individuals. I even told him the stories of the miraculous healings that I had witnessed. I also tried to point out to Brian that any healing of our physical bodies is, at best, very temporary, and is never guaranteed. I talked about Paul and we read 2 Corinthians 12:7-10 together. I talked about my own 40-year-long experience with Type 1 diabetes, which is killing me much more slowly than Brian's cancer was killing him. Brian's conviction remained strong and firm. He believed that being healed of this cancer was dependent on his own faith. (This can be, in my opinion, a misguided and hurtful teaching.) We visited, at length, more than a dozen times. I was truly amazed at his faith. I hoped that I would indeed see another miracle of God. I wanted to see Brian's earthly body healed of this cancer. He did, in fact, live much longer than the oncologists predicted. Brian fought bravely, and hoped valiantly, until the end.

Several weeks before the end came, however, I promised Brian that I would limit our conversations. I agreed to speak only words of faith, hope, and love to him. My last visit with Brian found him not able to speak at all, but he was still able to stay awake and seemed to be understanding. I read verses in the Old and New Testaments about God's love and power, grace and compassion. I also read verses about heaven and eternity with our Savior.

When God called Brian home to his eternal healing, I grieved his departure. I also grieved for his parents, whom I had come to know and love. I am not sure how much Brian might have learned from me, but I know I learned much from him.

It is **always** good to be gracious and to point to Jesus as our eternal hope.

6. Be very cautious with humor. Never be the first to use humor with the sick, the dying or the grieving. Also, please be aware that many patients, family, and friends will use humor as a way to hide or avoid their true feelings. I think men tend to do this more than women do. I would not condemn this avoidance mechanism when we see others use it, but it is good to be aware of and recognize it. You can then look for an opportunity to gently open a door for this person to encounter his grief and to talk about it, rather than to try to mask over it.

Someone who is grieving can easily feel devalued or even insulted if you and I come at them with humor. Some people don't understand or appreciate humor, even on a good day. Humor can also be cultural or even generational. This is not to condemn humor in general, as it can have a significant and helpful place. In most cases, a good funeral can have both tears and laughter. I would strongly advise against trying to use any humor at all in the funeral of a child, or in the funeral of a person whose death came under particularly tragic circumstances, such as murder or suicide. Again, I think a true story might be best to drive this point home.

I came to greatly value a dear older couple we will call Mr. and Mrs. Jones. He was about ten years older than she and they had been married for almost 60 years. She had been a school teacher and he had held a non-medical position of some importance in a hospital. When I met them, he had been retired for a long time, and was unsteady on his feet, to the point of struggling every time he had to stand. Although he had physical problems himself, he was determined to be there for his wife. With regular help from a nurse, an aide and their only son, Mr. Jones did an amazing job of caring for the love of his life.

Mrs. Jones had been receiving palliative care for several months, and her status had been fairly steady until her big decline came. It became clear that she had begun the early stages of the "active dying process." From my first visit with the Jones's, I knew that they were members of a small local church. Their pastor had a good ministerial education. I had not yet met him, but all that I had heard about him certainly sounded great.

I went to visit after this patient's final decline had begun, and Mr. Jones was very upset. I had never seen anger in this mild-mannered man before. With great emotion, he told me what had happened. Their pastor had come to visit earlier that same day. The minister had already been informed that Mrs. Jones had taken a significant turn for the worse and was non-responsive. The pastor, known for his jolly demeanor and great sense of humor, walked into the apartment singing a silly song. Before listening to anything that Mr. Jones had to say, the pastor had strolled into their home singing something funny and laughable — to a man who was actively grieving the approaching death of his wife.

Again, Mr. Jones was still steaming with anger hours after the pastor's brief visit was over. He told me that there was no way he was going to let their pastor do his wife's funeral. I listened to his anger and made no excuses for the pastor, but eventually asked Mr. Jones to be gracious and forgive his pastor's thoughtlessness. I asked Mr. Jones to remember their pastor's heart, the heart that he had come to know. Mrs. Jones died a couple of days later, and Mr. Jones did forgive his pastor. The pastor learned a valuable lesson, and I was honored to attend the funeral that he officiated.

7. Be generous with affirmation, in ministry and at home. Affirmation is a wonderful gift that tragically, I never even began to learn much about until I was 40 years old. Anyone can criticize and find fault with others, but those who can uplift, encourage and motivate others are truly special. As Christian ministers, we should be good at affirming others. Effective affirmers are given lucrative contracts in the business world and in sports at all levels. Most of the people who struggle with affirming others also tend to struggle with receiving affirmation from others.

Just like forgiveness is received and given to others, affirmation should be received and given to others. A truly humble person will receive affirmation with a smile and a thank you and then look for any possible way to affirm the one who just affirmed him. This did not come naturally to me. I had to consciously learn the art of affirmation, and I still have to remind myself to work at it. With continued practice, it does become more natural and even quite enjoyable.

In 1 Thessalonians 5:14 we are told, "Now we exhort you, brethren, warn those who are unruly, comfort the fainthearted, uphold the weak, be patient with all." If you find yourself focusing on the warning of the unruly, you probably need to learn more about what it means to comfort the fainthearted and uphold the weak, not to mention being patient with all of your patients.

If you notice that you often turn aside others' attempts to affirm you, and you also sometimes find yourself feeling a need for affirmation from others, then you are human and I am right there with you. You are one kind of "normal," and you probably need to work a little more on the whole area of confidence and humility, as we touched upon in the first section of this book.

Notice how Paul encouraged and affirmed others in Romans 1:7-8. "To all who are in Rome, beloved of God, called to be saints: Grace to you and peace from God our Father and the Lord Jesus Christ. First, I thank my God through Jesus Christ for you all, that your faith is spoken of throughout the whole world."

Then notice how the great apostle gives humble affirmation in verses 11-12, "For I long to see you, that I may impart to you some spiritual gift, so that you may be established; that is, that I may be encouraged together with you by the mutual faith both of you and me."

The final chapter of Romans is full of affirmation. Paul begins the chapter by commending Phoebe, the lady who carried this letter to Rome. Then in 16:3-4, it is Priscilla and Aquila's turn: "Greet Priscilla and Aquila, my fellow workers in Christ Jesus, who risked their own necks for my life, to whom not only I give thanks, but also all the churches of the Gentiles."

More affirmation comes in verses 6-7, "Greet Mary, who labored much for us. Greet Andronicus and Junia, my countrymen and my fellow prisoners, who are of note among the apostles, who also were in Christ before me."

Philippians 1:3-6 is classic: "I thank my God upon every remembrance of you, always in every prayer of mine making request for you all with joy, for your fellowship in the Gospel from the first day until now, being confident of this very thing, that He who has begun a good work in you will complete it until the day of Jesus Christ;"

In the last half of the final chapter to the Philippians, Paul mixes affirmation with thanks for the gift that the church at Philippi sent to him.

Talk about affirmation! Look at these verses again in 1 Thessalonians 1:2-3 & 6-9:

"We give thanks to God always for you all, making mention of you in our prayers, remembering without ceasing your <u>work of faith</u>, <u>labor of love</u>, and <u>patience of hope</u> in our Lord Jesus Christ in the sight of our God and Father,"

"And you became followers of us and of the Lord, having received the word in much affliction, with joy of the Holy Spirit, so that you became examples to all in Macedonia and Achaia who believe. For from you the word of the Lord has sounded forth, not only in Macedonia and Achaia, but also in every place. Your faith toward God has gone out, so that we do not need to say anything. For they themselves declare concerning us what manner of entry we had to you, and how you turned to God from idols to serve the living and true God."

2 Thessalonians 1:3-4 is perhaps not quite as familiar to our ears, but this is rich.

"We are bound to thank God always for you, brethren, as it is fitting, because your faith grows exceedingly, and the love of every one of you all abounds toward each other, so that we ourselves boast of you among the churches of God for your patience and faith in all your persecutions and tribulations that you endure…" (and it goes on further).

Other famously great encouragers include Barnabas and, of course, Jesus Himself.

Let me add two more quick notes that can relate to us today. When I meet someone whom I know is a veteran of our armed forces, and especially one of the few remaining WWII veterans, I always try to be sure to thank him or her for what they have done for our country. When we meet retired pastors or missionaries we should be eager and ready to give affirmation to them.

The other most important note is this: When you see family members and other loved ones caring for a patient, please take time to affirm them for the good work they are doing. Caring for a sick or dying person can be a very long, difficult and "thankless" job. The one they are caring for is usually too weak or too confused to thank them. Please be sure that their work does not go without affirmation from you.

It is almost always good to honestly affirm people. Anyone can criticize and find fault. ***Be one who can, and does, encourage and affirm.***

8. <u>Hear the Confessions of others</u>. Confession is, strangely, something we often tend to run from or dismiss. This point on confession is not in contradiction to affirmation. It is the honest recognition of the other side of our human situation. If a patient says, "Oh, I have been a terrible husband, losing my temper and …," our response may often be something like, "Oh, you probably are not all that bad." When someone has something to confess, he does indeed need to bring it before the Lord, but we should be there, ready to be of assistance. We need to be able to be quiet and listen. It is not our place to judge, ***nor is it our place to excuse or minimize the severity*** of what a person has done. I have heard some spectacular confessions but telling them here would be more entertaining than helpful. I also have a responsibility to keep almost all confessions confidential.

I do not feel that it is my place to interrogate anyone, but when someone offers a confession, we can humbly assist that person to bring his guilt before God. Sometimes we also may need to help a patient see that the guilt he may feel is probably unfounded. I realize this is a heavy responsibility. That is why we need to study God's word continually, and we need to prayerfully walk in the Spirit (2 Timothy 2:15 and Galatians 5:13-26).

I hope you are familiar with 1 John 1:9, "If we confess our sins, He is faithful and just to forgive us our sins and to cleanse us from all unrighteousness."

I also hope we have not forgotten the first part of James 5:16, "Confess your trespasses to one another, and pray for one another, that you may be healed."

I feel I should set forth one other verse here for your consideration. Galatians 6:1 says to us, "Brethren, if a man is overtaken in any trespass, you who are spiritual restore such a one in a spirit of gentleness, considering yourself lest you also be tempted.

I hope you can learn your proper and valuable role in acknowledging the needs of others to confess and being ready to be there with them as they do so. Again, most of this is simply listening and giving assurance of God's stated intention to forgive and to cleanse from sin (as we read above in 1 John 1:9).

Please remember the three important things that Galatians 6:1 gives us as instruction. We need to be spiritually prepared to do this task. We need to have a spirit of gentleness. We also need to be cautiously aware of our own vulnerability to sin.

9. <u>Keep what you have to share as simple as the situation calls for</u>. Most patients have limitations caused by their illness. The greater the pain or dementia or grief, the more it becomes necessary to keep the message simple. The sick and grieving are not in need of a great instructor or professor. They need a kind shepherd who cares for their soul.

In trying to be a kind shepherd, I make it my practice to read verses from the Bible almost every time I visit a patient. When the patient shows signs of great weakness and/or dementia, I try to use some of the more common passages that I hope my patient will recognize and possibly be familiar with. One can readily share the good news of the Gospel, reading such well-known passages as Psalm 23, the Beatitudes (Matthew 5), the Lord's Prayer (Matthew 6), and verses in John, chapters 3 and 10. I have often read the 23rd Psalm followed by John 10:11 & 27-30, both in regular visits and also in funeral services.

When you see that you really want to keep your message simple, this is the most uncomplicated two point outline I know:

1. God loves you. (He proved His love in the life, death and resurrection of Jesus.)
2. God really wants you to trust Him.

(There is certainly no shortage of verses that proclaim these wonderful points.)

Here is a story that I cannot say is typical, but it is what God did, and it serves as one example of when to keep things simple. This story also says something about confession.

I went out to visit a patient for the first time. She was in her mid-thirties, and she had been told by her physicians that cancer would end her life in only a few weeks, at most. When I arrived for this visit, it was very clear that the Lord was already working in this young lady's heart. Right after some very brief introductions, she said to me with great emotion, "There is no way the Lord can forgive me for all the horrible things I have done, is there?" She had been addicted to drugs for most of her life. She apparently had done most of the unfortunate things that drug addicts tend to do in order to get the substances that feed their addiction.

This woman probably could have gone on and on confessing, but that was really not necessary at this point. She knew she wanted forgiveness, but feared that it was too late for her. I did not minimize her actions. I did tell her that God had been willing to forgive David, who had stolen another man's wife and then committed murder. I also told her that God had forgiven Paul, who had been responsible for the arrests and deaths of innocent believers. I turned to 1 John 1:9 and read it to her. (We just read this same verse a couple of pages back.) I told her that I believed she was sincere. I read this straightforward verse again and told her that I believed God loved her and wanted to give her forgiveness and peace. I prayed a brief, prayer for her and then invited her to pray to the Lord. She spoke the most beautiful, heartfelt prayer I could ever imagine.

This young woman pleaded for and received forgiveness and peace from our Lord and Savior. I could have sat down with her and tried to teach all about total depravity, the vicarious atonement, the proper understanding of baptism and all about church polity, but I believe all that was totally unnecessary. God had already been working his wonderful grace into her life, and I was just blessed to be the one who got to witness what God was doing. In the following days this dear soul testified of her faith to others, and two weeks later she died. God gave her love joy and peace and I got to watch.

10. <u>Be a rock, but do not be a landslide</u>. Do not just march in and take charge. Look, listen and assess the situation. Practice compassionate pastoral presence. Be the solid, confident presence of faith and hope. Observe the family; see where they are, and what they seem to be going through. Pray for discernment in order to determine the extent of your role. The seat next to the sick or dying patient does not belong to you (maybe for just a few minutes). Unless you are alone with the patient, that closest chair belongs to the spouse, the children, or the parent. The better you know the family, the more prominent your role will probably be. Different family and friends might have very different expectations of you. Again, do not take advantage of or bully others in their time of grief. Give comfort, encouragement, and hope. Acknowledge their grief and recognize that their grief is normal and proper. Again, I want to expand and clarify these words of instruction with a personal story.

A home patient we will call Teresa was dying of cancer. She was a very young-looking forty-year-old mother of two teenaged children. Teresa had put her faith in Christ and become active in her church only about a year before. I had been to visit with Teresa a couple of times when she was able to share her thoughts and her faith with me. The time came, however, when it was clear that Teresa was actively dying. I went to visit Teresa in her home one day, and I was fairly certain that she would die that day.

There were about twenty family members and friends gathered in and around their small, poorly constructed duplex. Teresa was non-responsive, lying in a hospital bed that was placed in the living room. Her own mother, sister, and brothers, and her two daughters were rotating in and out of those chairs closest to her bedside. I went to be with this family, listening individually to some and also leading them together in prayer a couple of times.

Then Teresa's pastor arrived, along with his wife and another woman from the church. This pastor was an outgoing people person, but he took little time at all to stop and listen to this grieving family. He announced his presence, took his position at the foot of the bed, said a nice big prayer and began singing with his guitar. His wife and the other woman backed him up with some pretty good harmonies. The patient's family and the pastor were all Hispanic so there was no apparent cultural gap, but no one in the room seemed to know the songs other than the pastor and his two backup singers. They sang three or four long songs, then without a pause in the performance, the pastor began to preach. My Spanish is limited, but it sounded like he was preaching the Gospel, and he mentioned death and dying.

It was all so overwhelming. There seemed to be little, if any, acknowledgment of what was happening. There was no listening to the very real grief of the family. There was another platform kind of prayer and then there was more singing. I had already been there about two hours and I had other patients scheduled to see who were not very far away. I told one of the family members that I needed to go, but I would still be in the area. And so I slipped out while the pastor was still singing.

It was a little more than an hour later that I got a call from one of our nurses, reporting that Teresa had died. I hurried over to the house where the family was showing their grief with a lot of tears and weeping. I realized that the pastor and his entourage were no longer present, so I asked the patient's sister when they had left. She said they had been gone for less than a half hour. She also said, "We are not calling him back over here." I went about my task of listening to grieving family members and weeping with those who wept. With so many people present, it would have been very nice to have a few more ministers to give caring support. I stayed until about an hour later, when the funeral directors came to remove Teresa's lifeless body. I led in a prayer, thanking God for His grace given to Teresa. I also asked the Lord to help these grieving loved ones.

I wished that the pastor had known more about listening to and showing love to this grieving family. I feel that he could have been used in such a great way if he had been more of a gentle shepherd to these grieving souls. It seems that he wasted a wonderful opportunity to personally show God's love and compassion to them.

11. <u>Learn to deal with discouraging circumstances</u>. What we see around us often hammers home the reality of the depravity of man, but please do not forget the amazing power and sufficiency of the grace of God.

Many times the most discouraging thing for me is when people who seem to need help the most are the very ones who refuse to allow me, or anyone else, to come and minister to them. Certainly, as a chaplain, I cannot barge in when uninvited. You, who are likely involved in some local church ministry, might well have fewer restrictions on you than I do as I go out as a chaplain. Even so, neither one of us need to be doing any "barging." Even God Himself very rarely forces His way in. What freedom we humans have is too often used to reject the help that we each need. My heart is often broken for those who, proclaiming their own independence, refuse to welcome a kind offer of compassion and hope. The good news is that no one can keep us from praying. We should never forget the potential power of a prayer that is clearly in line with God's love and grace.

Please remember that those to whom we minister are each hurting and frail human beings. Times of illness, death, and grief can sometimes bring out the best in people. Such times can also bring out the worst in people. Often family members, who may have been estranged for years, are suddenly brought together to the same place, and many times it gets messy. I have seen family feuds and fights that have gotten ugly, and very sad.

I remember one occasion in a hospital. I was called and arrived just before the security guys got there. Just outside the ICU, a daughter and the sister of a patient were yelling at one another. Male family members were standing alongside each of these women, ready to come to blows if their side did not get its way. About all I did was let them know that I was listening, and encouraged them to talk rather than fight. It was the security guys who probably kept it from becoming violent that day.

A little later, I had an opportunity to speak one-on-one with "Debbie", the daughter of the patient. She told me her story. There was a long-running feud between her mother, the terminally ill patient in the ICU, and her mother's sister (Debbie's aunt). Sometime before, perhaps when the mother was first hospitalized, she had told Debbie to not even let her sister in the room. Debbie had promised that she would not ever let her come in. Now the patient was minimally responsive and Debbie's aunt wanted to see her dying sister. I kindly asked Debbie to consider giving her mother and her aunt one last chance to make peace. Debbie stuck to her guns and said she would not. She insisted that she had made a promise to her mother.

The next day, I was across the ICU area seeing another patient when I saw the aunt step into her sister's room. Soon after, Debbie went into the room. At that point, all I could do was pray. A few minutes later I looked across the way again and saw Debbie and her aunt outside the patient's room. They were hugging one another and both seemed to be sobbing. Forgiveness and love had won the day, but that is not always the way it goes.

Be very cautious about taking sides in family fights. Also, try not to let yourself get emotionally involved when family members get into conflicts, whether with one another or with caregivers or medical staff. Remember that we usually only get one side of a story the first time we listen. We need to try to be the calm foundation of reason. Even when one side of a dispute seems to hold the moral high ground over the other, we need to maintain fairness and grace and pray for the wisdom of Solomon. Remember also that you are not the judge. You, hopefully, can represent integrity and justice, but you have no real power to enforce justice. Eventually, we must believe that God will. Again, please remember to hold 2 Timothy 2:23-26 & Romans 12:17-21 as a standard for yourself.

A couple more observations:

When a widow or widower remarries and then is dying; his or her children will very seldom support the new spouse, even if the couple has been married for 10 or 20 years. Many, many times they will turn against him or especially, against her. Often the reason for this has to do with money and possessions to be inherited, but it is not just about the money. Old feelings and emotions tend to come up again. The adult children often feel that the new spouse should not be there replacing their deceased parent. If the situation has come about because of divorce rather than the death of a parent, emotions are even more likely to be ugly. I have seen this happen so often that I just expect the need to deal with a lot of hurt feelings and discord in these situations. I also pray for wisdom. You and I cannot make people feel the way that we think they should feel. We can always, and should always, pray. We can try to be an anchor in the storm and, as you know, we should do our best to speak the truth in love.

Here is a reminder that should help in dealing with discouragement. **You are who God says you are**. Many will reject you or discount your ministry as foolish or useless. Don't believe them. Others might occasionally hail you as the next Mother Teresa or Billy Graham. Please don't believe them either. You are the one that God made you to be. He wants to use you. He has a purpose and a plan for you. Don't let circumstances or mere mortals turn you away from these truths.

A few years ago I had what turned out to be a long and very remarkable day in the big city near my home. After leaving our office, I drove to see a lady who was cared for by family members in her apartment. I had only been to see this lady once before. She had been somewhat confused at the first visit, but this day was going to be a little different. This patient's family was concerned about her and they hoped that a chaplain might be helpful. I stepped into the patient's room, reminded her that I was the chaplain that had come once before. I wanted to get a feeling for where she was emotionally and spiritually. The patient did not express much understanding but seemed to become restless and anxious. Then I heard her plainly say to me, "You're the devil." After a moment of surprise, I responded, "Uh, no, I'm the chaplain who came a week or two ago. You've met me before. I work with your nurse, Johnnie." To which she replied, "No, I know who you are. You are the devil!"

I quickly realized that arguing would not do any good here. I also saw that my presence was actually making things worse instead of better, so I backed away with some kind, reassuring words. I retreated to the next room and told the patient's sister exactly what had happened. She was almost as shocked as I was. I listened to the sister and another caregiver for a while as a third lady went in to try her hand at comforting the patient. The sister and friend were able to reflect a bit on the patient's confusion and continuing decline. I hoped I had perhaps helped the family members some, but I was pretty sure I had not been any help at all to the patient. A few days later I was told that for that entire day, this patient had thought every man she saw was the devil.

This same day, however, I went on to make a couple of other visits then, well after dark, I arrived at the home of a family in the same city. A father in his forties was dying of gastrointestinal cancer. This visit was a second- or third-time visit with them. The patient had a wife and together they had a couple of teenagers. This man was already in the actively dying stage. The doctor and nurses had worked hard for days to get him comfortable, and it was still somewhat of a struggle.

The wife was very anxious and had probably not slept for more than a few hours over the past several days. She was one who could hardly leave her husband's side, and her anticipatory grief did not seem to be going in a healthy direction. I stayed for about an hour, sitting with the patient and encouraging the daughter and the son to share some of their thoughts and emotions. I also tried to help them reflect a little on the unknown timing of their father's coming death. The wife also took part in this visit a little. I said a few verses from the Bible and offered a prayer, asking God to give comfort and grace to both patient and family.

It was one of those visits when I hated to leave them, but it seemed the right time to go. I also had about an hour's drive ahead of me to get home. The wife followed me out the front door into the yard and put her hand on my arm. She looked me straight in the eye and said, "I know who you are, you are Jesus." This time, I know my jaw dropped, as I said, "Uh, what? " Then I called her by name and said, "You know that I am just a chaplain. I have been here before to visit with you and your husband."

Again she insisted, "No, you sound like Jesus, you look like Jesus. I know who you are. Please, Jesus, take my husband to heaven. I can't just keep watching him suffer any longer." I responded to her tearful request, "I am not Jesus, but we can talk to Jesus right now." We bowed our heads together and I prayed that Jesus would indeed hear her desperate cry for help. After praying, I reminded this dear lady that she had others there to help her, others who could sit with her husband. I told her she desperately needed to sleep.

As the day came to a close, the one lady probably still thought I was the devil and the second lady might have still thought I was Jesus. Strangely, I was much more shaken by being identified as Jesus than I was being called the devil. Driving home that night I had time to consider these two very opposite cases of confusion about who I was.

It is important that each of us stays grounded on the truth of who we really are. You and I are each someone God has created; a human being who has stepped out in faith, now trying to help others in their times of greatest need and frequent confusion. We cannot do what only God can do. Some of those you encounter may, on some days, think you must be the devil himself. Other times, you may be hailed as someone far above who you really are. What matters is what God thinks of you. Ask Him, and He will give you all the grace that you will ever need. 2 Corinthians 9:8 has got to be one of the most encouraging verses in the Bible.

"And God is able to make all grace abound toward you, that you, always having all sufficiency in all things, may have an abundance for every good work."

12. <u>Examine yourself to be sure that you are not carrying around any discrimination or prejudice</u>. I do mean racial prejudice, but I do not only mean racial prejudice. Prejudice is a widespread problem that is almost always quickly denied by anyone suspected of it. The Scriptures have enough statements in them that we need not wonder about God's position here.

Deuteronomy 10:17 says "For the LORD your God is God of gods and Lord of lords, the great God, mighty and awesome, who <u>shows no partiality</u> nor takes a bribe. He administers justice for the fatherless and the widow, <u>and loves the stranger (also translated, "foreigner")</u>, giving him food and clothing. Therefore <u>love the stranger, for you were strangers</u> in the land of Egypt."

Acts 10:34 speaks of Cornelius and Peter in the same way. "Then Peter opened his mouth and said 'In truth, I perceive that God shows no partiality. But in every nation whoever fears Him and works righteousness is accepted by Him.'"

In Acts 15:7-9 we read this account of Peter before the Jerusalem conference, "Peter rose up and said to them: 'Men and brethren, you know that a good while ago God chose among us, that by my mouth the Gentiles should hear the word of the Gospel and believe. So God, who knows the heart, acknowledged them by giving them the Holy Spirit, just as He did us, and made no distinction between us and them, purifying their hearts by faith.'"

Unless you were born into a Jewish family, you are one of the vast majority of people who could be called "outsiders." But God chose, in Christ, to eliminate the whole idea of "outsiders." That is what we just read in the books of Deuteronomy and Acts. You probably are very familiar with John 1:11-12:

"He (Jesus) came unto His own, and His own did not receive Him. But as many as received Him, to them He gave the right to become children of God, to those who believe in His name."

Romans 2:11: "For there is no partiality with God."

Romans 10:12: "For there is no distinction between Jew and Greek, for the same Lord over all is rich to all who call upon Him."

1 Peter 2:17: "<u>Honor</u> all *people*. Love the brotherhood. Fear God. <u>Honor</u> the king."

With our vast and varied "middle class", most of us have a hard time grasping the full strength of the following words given to a world that mostly had just the rich and the poor.

James 2:1-9 says "My brethren, do not hold the faith of our Lord Jesus Christ, the Lord of glory, with partiality. For if there should come into your assembly a man with gold rings, in fine apparel, and there should also come in a poor man in filthy clothes, and you pay attention to the one wearing the fine clothes and say to him, "You sit here in a good place," and say to the poor man, "You stand there," or, Sit here at my footstool," have you not shown partiality among yourselves, and become judges with evil thoughts? Listen, my beloved brethren: Has God not chosen the poor of this world to be rich in faith and heirs of the kingdom which He promised to those who love Him? But you have dishonored (We would say 'disrespected' today.) the poor man. Do not the rich oppress you and drag you into the courts? Do they not blaspheme that noble name by which you are called? If you really fulfill the royal law according to the Scripture, "You shall love your neighbor as yourself," you do well; but if you show partiality, you commit sin, and are convicted by the law as transgressors."

In writing about this topic, I found myself wanting to get all theoretical and preachy, but I really don't think that is necessary. I continue to presume that you, the reader, are a sincere follower of Jesus Christ. The verses given above are more than clear enough. I think that if you need more said to convince you, then we are really in trouble. I will say that I asked myself, along with several others, why any person would be racist and bigoted against another person whom they see as different from themselves. The most prominent reasons noted were pride, ignorance, fear, and selfishness. I think that fear and ignorance tend to go together, as do the pride and selfishness.

Pride was apparently the first sin and it seems to me that I see more outward, shameless pride today than at any other time in my life. In many ways, racial discrimination has decreased greatly since the 1950's and 60's, but please do not think that racism is gone from the United States, or from any other country for that matter. If we honestly observe the people around us, we will see that racial bigotry and even hatred are still easy to find. Our first job in this regard is to humbly examine our own hearts and look at our own attitudes and actions. You have probably noticed that it is hard to change the hearts of others, but it is much less difficult to sincerely ask God to change our own hearts.

If you find yourself ministering in an area with different cultures and peoples, seek out opportunities to truly befriend people of these various cultures and people groups. If they speak a different language, maybe you can learn enough to read from the Bible in their language. Maybe you can learn a prayer or a song or two in their language. The more you get to know a people, the less "different" they will seem to you, and that is a very good thing.

Remember the first word on the list of reasons why people become prejudiced? It was fear. So, Fear not. God is with you and He wants to use you to love your neighbor.

A good name is better than precious ointment, And the day of death than the day of one's birth;

Better to go to the house of mourning than to go to the house of feasting, For that is the end of all men; And the living will take it to heart.

Sorrow is better than laughter, For by a sad countenance the heart is made better.

The heart of the wise is in the house of mourning, But the heart of fools is in the house of mirth.

It is better to hear the rebuke of the wise than for a man to hear the song of fools.

Ecclesiastes 7:1-5

VI

SITUATIONS

Situations according to place:

<u>Visiting a patient in a hospital room</u>
When you visit a patient in a hospital you are a guest in a medical facility. The hospital staff and physicians have the primary focus of treating and protecting their patient. There is always some kind of visiting hours, along with other limitations that are primarily for the good of the patients. In most situations, your visit will be welcomed as good and helpful, especially if you respect the rules of the hospital and if you respect all the staff who work in the hospital. You are a guest. The staff members are not the enemy and neither are the rules. If one day they somehow become the enemy, what did Jesus tell us to do with our enemies? Yes, we are to love them and bless them and forgive them.

Why do I say all of this? Well, because I have seen some visiting ministers who seem to have some strange attitudes. Hospitals can inspire some uncomfortable emotions and behavior in people. For many, even for some Christian ministers, hospitals may be scary or intimidating places. Perhaps this comes from past experiences or from stories heard from others. If you had some difficult or even terrible hospital experience, you might do well to talk to someone about it, to see if you can make some sense of what that experience meant to you. Past tragedies will certainly affect us, but they do not need to control our attitudes today. For most of us, the more time we spend in a hospital, the more we will feel comfortable there.

You can usually find out the various visiting hours and other hospital rules by asking at the front entry desk, or by calling the main hospital phone number. Both of these sources should be able to tell you if a patient is currently in the hospital, and if so, they can give you the patient's location. That is about all that they can tell you though, because of the HIPAA rules (Health Insurance Portability and Accountability Act of 1996). However, if the patient happens to be in a psychiatric ward or is designated as a possible victim of abuse, the staff may not even be allowed to tell you if the patient is currently in the hospital.

When you come to the hospital floor where your patient is located, there is almost always a nurses' desk in a central location on that floor. If you are visiting a patient for the first time on this floor, it is usually a good idea to just casually tell someone at the desk who you are and that you, for example, have come to visit Mrs. Susan Smith in room 204. You are not really asking permission to visit. You are opening communication, showing respect and kindness. If, perchance, there is some reason why you should not visit that particular patient at that particular time, the nurse or another staff person will probably let you know. If there are some special restrictions regarding the patient, you will likely be told at this point.

Now you arrive at the door of the patient's room. There are two important things to remember before touching that door knob. First of all, please notice and read whatever messages might be posted on or next to the door. Sometimes there is a warning about some kind of infection control. Occasionally a sign will be there to say that anyone entering the room must first put on gloves, a mask, a protective gown, or all of the above. You will be told what to put on, and the required items should all be located right there beside the door, tightly stuffed into little cardboard boxes. This may seem like a huge bother, but it is important to comply with such requirements. It is meant to protect you, and it may even be required to protect the patient.

Then, all the protective gear you put on when you entered will need to be taken off and discarded in a big marked container just before you leave the room. Turn your gloves wrong side out as you remove them, only touching the inside of the gloves, not the outside. You will get better at this, or at least quicker, with experience. You can practice at home with some latex or plastic gloves from the store if you want. Remember to laugh at yourself, especially if you have to wear one of those "duck masks."

When you have read any notices on the door and complied with the directions, it is time to knock rather loudly and then wait to hear a voice before entering. Listen to what the voice has to say. If you cannot hear, then open the door slightly, just so you can hear, but not see. The last thing you want to do is embarrass the patient and yourself by walking in at a time when the patient needs privacy. Think about how you would feel if you were the patient, and the day after your surgery a church member walked in while a nurse was helping you to get on the bedside commode!

Even in the best of circumstances, you will usually want to keep your hospital visits fairly brief. If the patient is recovering from surgery or some kind of infection, he will tire quickly, and he will need a lot of rest. Five to fifteen minutes is usually plenty of time. In some circumstances, a patient or family member might need someone to sit with him for a longer period of time. It is almost always important to offer up a prayer during your visit, and the prayer does not have to come at the end of the visit. It can be good to pray near the beginning of the visit. It is certainly good to say or read an appropriate portion of Scripture during your visit. We will talk more about choosing verses later.

Speak kind words to the staff members you meet. Thank them and affirm them for their work if this is at all appropriate. They are physically taking care of the one that you care about. When a physician or a nurse comes into the room, introduce yourself, and tell them you will be glad to step out to let them do their part with the patient. If the doctor needs to tell the patient some information or test results, you should step out of the room unless the patient clearly asks you to stay to hear what the doctor has to say. Again, there are HIPAA rules that prohibit the doctor and staff members from sharing a patient's medical information with you unless the patient or the patient's medical power of attorney specifically says that you should hear the information. This has been the law for several years now. By offering to step out of the room, you show the medical staff that you respect the law, and you respect their need to comply with the law. The patient can certainly tell you whatever she wants to tell you after the doctor leaves, but please do not put the medical people in a situation where they have to ask you to leave.

Please forgive me if I say or even repeat some obvious realities. You will never catch cancer by visiting cancer patients in the hospital. Most hospital patients are no more contagious than any other people we meet on the street every day. However, I should point out that hospital staff, and all chaplains, are taught to "observe universal precautions." This basically means that we always presume every patient could have AIDS or Hepatitis C. So we avoid letting our skin come in contact with a patient's blood or other body fluids. There are a lot of infectious diseases out there, and most patients do not just have one disease. Please be practical and use common sense, but do not be micro phobic. I worked in a hospital full-time for over three years, and never caught anything from a patient. I only wore gloves and a mask when ordered to do so. For over a dozen years I have visited dying people, well over 40 hours a week, in homes, nursing facilities and many hospitals. I have gotten older, but I have not gotten sicker. So do not fret; just use common sense and press on.

In an ICU, CCU or another such special care area of a hospital
Usually, in an intensive care unit of a hospital, there are more restrictive visiting hours. If you try to go around these rules without permission, security people might come and help you. Help you to leave the building, that is. If the rules are telling you to stay out, but you are sure that you really need to see a particular patient anyway, there is still hope. Be sure to use words of kindness to explain the situation to the charge nurse as you ask for permission to see the patient. Please don't threaten with some divine authority. God is always in charge. You and I are not, of course, and that's okay.

ICU patients are usually more ill and less able to respond than other hospital patients. Generally, one nurse will be assigned to just two or three patients, and the nurse will be properly protective of his or her patients.

Once you have come into the unit, it is usually a good idea to ask someone at the central desk if you can speak with your patient's particular nurse before you visit with that patient. There is often a person at the central desk of the ICU who serves more as a secretary than a nurse. He or she is usually there to coordinate things and help with communication and record keeping. This person might tell you that your patient's nurse is busy with another patient, and he or she might well be able to tell you whatever you need to know before you go in to visit the patient. Here again, you might be required to put on a mask and gloves and maybe even a gown. Such requirements are more likely to be needed in an ICU than in other areas of the hospital.

Sometimes an ICU patient is assessed as being in a terminal condition. If the patient is expected to die in a relatively short period of time and further aggressive treatment would be futile, such a patient will often be transferred to something more like a regular hospital room. If the hospital has a palliative care unit, the patient will likely be taken there. Some hospitals have a whole area just for inpatient hospice care. Palliative care is really what hospice care is all about. The goal is to comfort the patient as well as possible when there are no more curative options for the patient that have any reasonable chance of being effective. Sometimes a terminal patient will need to stay in the ICU. This could be because the patient's condition is seen as too fragile for her to be moved. If a patient is dying in the ICU, the rules regarding how many visitors are allowed in the room or even times of visitation may possibly be adjusted. This would be so that family and closest friends could be with the dying patient. Some hospitals will be stricter with their rules than others.

Many patients go straight to an ICU or a CCU (Cardiac Care Unit) for a day or more after a major surgery. Victims of poisoning usually go to an ICU, as do most of those who have attempted suicide. Mobile phone use is usually prohibited in an ICU and also in some other areas of most hospitals.

In the ER

Most ERs are not really like we see in television shows. There is usually a waiting room with a lot of patients and their families. They are all very eager to be seen by the medical staff as soon as possible. An ER might be "quiet" for a while, but the staff will not want you to use that word. The superstitious nature of many will think that using words such as "quiet" or "slow" might cause a flood of incoming patients. A busy ER can be a stressful and difficult place. Usually, when you arrive to see a patient in the ER, that patient has already arrived before you. If you don't see your patient or her family members sitting in the waiting area, go to the check-in desk, stand in line if there is one, introduce yourself and tell the attendant which patient you are there to see. You will usually be given some kind of badge or wristband showing that you are a visitor in the ER, and you will be told where to find your patient. Most ERs have some kind of security personnel there as well, especially at night. Most of the normal hospital rules apply, but know that things move at a faster pace. It is often a matter of "hurry up and wait." Those who bring themselves to the ER go through the waiting room and a triage nurse. A triage nurse's job is to prioritize the incoming patients. He or she will decide who goes straight on back, and who can wait. Do not try to become part of this decision-making process. Those designated to make such decisions know that people's lives may depend on their judgment calls. The most intervening thing I might do in an ER waiting room, and have done, is to encourage the patient to clearly tell the staff about each of his or her symptoms. Sometimes people do not want to talk about their symptoms, or they seem to think that doctors and nurses can figure everything out on their own, but it could be dangerous for the patient not to tell the medical staff everything that could be pertinent to his illness or injury.

When their turn comes, the patient is thrilled to be taken from the waiting area to an ER room, but then the patient usually has to wait quite a while longer before being seen by a nurse, and then by a physician, as there are far more nurses than there are doctors. ER staff members tend to be a special kind of professionals. They have limited time with each patient, and they really do not want you, me or anyone else to slow them down or get in their way. You and your patient will have to wait for them, but do not make the medical staff have to wait on you. When a nurse or a physician arrives in your patient's room, do not hesitate to step aside so they can do their part for your patient. Our job in the ER is mainly to be a support and comfort to the patient and family. They have landed here because of an emergency. Their world may have just been turned upside down. They are probably in pain and probably afraid. They need your steady, loving, prayerful presence.

If you have come to see a true trauma patient — someone who came in with serious physical injuries or something such as a heart attack, respiratory distress or a stroke — they probably came by ambulance and will bypass the waiting room. When someone is in critical condition, needing immediate treatment to try to save their life, they normally go straight to a trauma room. We don't get to sit in a trauma room. Family members and friends of these patients are usually brought to a "family room." When I worked in a hospital as the chaplain on call and heard, "Code blue in the ER," I dropped everything, wherever I was, and hurried to the ER family room. Family members were either already there, or they arrived just after I did. If you are a pastor to the patient and arrive at the ER asking about a patient who has been sent to a trauma room, you will likely be sent to the family room along with the patient's family and closest friends. Just be sure to tell the person at the ER desk of your relationship to the patient.

I am going to tell you what I would typically do when called to the ER as the chaplain on call. Your role as a pastor is mostly the same, except that the family probably knows you already. I would tell the friends and family who I was and invite them to tell me what was happening. If you do not know who is who, try to remember who the key people are in relationship to the patient. Words almost always come fast and furious, as these very anxious people each tell their version of what they think has happened to their loved one. Sometimes when I arrived, the family members wanted to go see their loved one right away. I would tell them that the medical staff was working aggressively to help their loved one, and we needed to just wait and pray until the doctor came to report to us. Being one of the hospital chaplains, I sometimes received information about the patient before arriving in the family room, but most of the time I only knew as much as the family members knew. Even when I had some medical information about the patient, I knew it was not my place to give that information to them. I am not a physician or a nurse. I do not understand enough about medical issues to give out or explain medical information correctly. We really need to be cautious, because we can easily add to the confusion if we try to be someone we are not. I waited with the family, usually prayed with them, and always listened to them. This is a time to be steady, compassionate and patient. Sometimes the wait is long, and what you are waiting for is either a word of hope or a word of very bad news.

The best scenario is when the doctor comes in with a look of some relief on his face. He introduces himself to the family members and usually gives some kind of diagnosis. He tells of treatment done and tells the family where the patient is going next. Often the patient is going to an ICU or CCU and may still be in serious or critical condition.

Another scenario is when the doctor and a nurse come in together, with very uncomfortable faces. I always knew what the news would be as soon as I saw their faces. The doctor takes a close family member by the hand, usually gets at eye level with them, and says something like, "I am sorry Mrs. Jones. We did all we could, but we could not save your husband's life. He appears to have had a severe heart attack (just as an example), and he has died." The doctor and nurse will normally stay only a minute or two, to answer the most basic questions if they can, and then they have to go help other patients.

If there is a hospital chaplain available when a patient dies in the ER, this chaplain will probably come to the family room too. The chaplain can probably stay there to help with the family for a while. If the chaplain is needed elsewhere, he or she might thank you for being there to help the family and then go to the next place of need. If the chaplain can stay, that is usually a very good thing. Often there are lots of friends and family coming when they hear that their loved one has come to the ER. In such group grief situations, two ministers are better than one. This is not a place for any kind of competition. This is a place where a lot of people may need someone to show compassion to them, listen to them and pray for them. Even in a group of people, you will mostly be listening to one or two at a time. You will sometimes also need to lead all of them together in prayer. By the way, if these people are part of your church, they will never forget that you were there with them. They will probably not remember what you said to them, but they will remember that you were there and that you love them. When I was the hospital chaplain and a church pastor arrived, I was glad to follow his lead. If he did not seem to have a clue as to what he should do, as was sometimes the case, I tried to respectfully be helpful in any way that was appropriate. Hospital chaplains are generally taught to defer to a patient's own pastor.

In a nursing or rehabilitation facility
Patients in nursing homes usually stay there for a much longer time than patients in hospitals do. You usually get to visit with them a little longer too. It is good to initiate some contact with the staff in this setting as well. The nursing home staff will tend to appreciate your visits to their patients even more than the typical hospital staff does. They also tend to be less protective in the sense of being difficult. There is a lot of loneliness in nursing homes, and there never seems to be enough staff members to give each patient as much help or attention as they need. There is a lot of waiting, and patients are usually glad to have a visitor. It seems that pastors are more likely to visit their church members in the hospital than in a nursing home, which is unfortunate.

There are patients at all levels of physical and mental ability in nursing homes. Some are there for rehabilitation after a surgery or an injury. Most patients are there long-term and many will spend their final days there. People often say that they would never send their family member off to a nursing facility, but many of these same people find out that they are not able to meet their family member's needs in any other way. Some facilities are much better than others. Some are expensive and rather exclusive. Others take in those with the least of means. Sometimes the place with the most modern, beautiful building is not actually the best place to be a patient. The biggest difference is made by the management setting the standards and the people they hire to implement them. A well-run nursing home will not smell of urine, and the staff members will do their jobs conscientiously and with compassion.

Nursing facilities are usually places of great need. If you know people there, please visit them with some regularity. You will also find that such a facility is a great place for you to do a lot of on-the-job training. You will gain invaluable experience. You will learn more than you ever thought you would and, in the process, the patients will be blessed. Sometimes gracious people come from a church to hold regular services in a facility. This can be a great encouragement, but I wish more people could spend the time to simply sit with these precious people one-on-one, and listen to the needs of their hearts.

Sometimes the patient you visit will seem to only want to complain about everything; at those times, it is good to listen with compassion. Acknowledge the patient's hardships, and eventually, you might find a blessing to focus on. Do not try to just cheer up those who weep. Remember Romans 12:15; "Weep with those who weep", and do not scold patients who complain. I try to move toward some realistic understanding of the patient's situation. I want to remind each patient that the Lord knows exactly what she is going through (Psalm 31:7), and the Lord still loves her as much as He ever has. Sometimes the best way to show a lonely, discouraged patient that God still cares is to allow God to care for that patient through you. You are there as some measure of proof that God has not forgotten them.

A private home
"There is no place like home"; so said Dorothy in the Wizard of Oz. There is some deep truth to that statement. Usually, when I visit a patient at home for the first time, I ask them how long they have lived there. If the patient has only been there for a few years, they might still be thinking of someplace else as home, so then I usually ask them where they grew up as a child. Visiting in a person's home is very different from visiting them in any kind of facility. I usually just arrive at a reasonable time when visiting a patient in a nursing home. When visiting a patient in his own home, however, I always try to call beforehand and make an appointment. I really do not like to call and schedule appointments, but I do it, nonetheless.

There is another well-known saying, "A man's home is his castle," and that goes for women just the same. In a private home, the patient and family are hosts and, again, we are the guests. It is always nice to affirm a person or family by noticing and mentioning something positive about their home. If you, however, really cannot honestly find something complimentary to say, then forcing something would probably just sound fake. It is sometimes easy for an at-home visit to go longer than you intended, so be cautious about this. Even if everyone was having a great time for an hour or two, it is possible that someone is going to regret all of the time that was spent. If we stay too long the first time, there may never be a second time. It is good to have a little one-on-one session with God before each visit, no matter where you go to see a patient. Part of your prayer might be a request for guidance as to how long you should stay. Sometimes upon leaving, I have realized that I have stayed too long.

Be kindly affectionate to one another with brotherly love, in honor giving preference to one another;

not lagging in diligence, fervent in spirit, serving the Lord;

rejoicing in hope, patient in tribulation, continuing steadfastly in prayer;

distributing to the needs of the saints, given to hospitality.

Bless those who persecute you; bless and do not curse.

Rejoice with those who rejoice, and weep with those who weep.

Be of the same mind toward one another. Do not set your mind on high things, but associate with the humble. Do not be wise in your own opinion.

Repay no one evil for evil. Have regard for good things in the sight of all men.

If it is possible, as much as depends on you, live peaceably with all men.

Beloved, do not avenge yourselves, but rather give place to wrath; for it is written, "Vengeance is Mine, I will repay." says the Lord.

Therefore

"If your enemy is hungry, feed him;

If he is thirsty, give him a drink;

For in so doing you will heap coals of fire on his head."

Do not be overcome by evil, but overcome evil with good."

Romans 12:10-21

Situations listed according to patient's particular condition:

<u>A patient who is minimally responsive or non-responsive</u>
When you are called upon to visit a patient who cannot speak to you, there is usually still some hope that the patient can hear. Try to find out this person's history of hearing ability. If the patient has been quite deaf for years and now is minimally responsive, her hearing will not have improved. She is still deaf, but you can hold her hand, pray for her, or use a picture board and/or a notepad if she can still see. If communication with your patient is just not possible, you will probably want to focus primarily on the patient's family and friends. If your non-verbal patient was hearing when she was still verbal, then she likely can still hear as well now as she could then. I recently visited a lady over 100 years of age. The patient was non-responsive, but her roommate told me she knew the patient could hear just fine a couple of weeks before, so I went ahead and read Scriptures and sang a couple of old hymns to her. If your patient's hearing has been impaired for some time, check on the availability and functionality of their hearing aids, if they had them. Hearing aids can be a big frustration. They malfunction, batteries get lost, and in nursing facilities, they often get thrown out with the trash (they make for very expensive trash). Hearing aids really can be a great help when they are available and in working order, though. I usually keep a headset and amplifier device in my car that I occasionally use to help with hard-of-hearing patients who have no hearing aids.

Now let's say you find yourself with a nonverbal and minimally responsive, but probably hearing, patient. You will be the only one talking. I would recommend that you fairly quickly come to what is most meaningful. After some kind, respectful words of greeting, you can acknowledge the patient's obvious limitations. You might want to acknowledge a little of what you know about the patient's life, faith, and family. Then, it is time to read some Scripture. If you know anything about what the patient's favorite passages are, those may be the best place to start. If the patient's old Bible is visible, take a look inside. If she has marked her Bible in any way, rejoice and read to her what has already touched her heart. Most of the time, however, I don't find a marked Bible lying in the room, so I usually start with some of the great Psalms. Psalms 13, 23, 27, 31, 32, 33, 34, 46, 51, 71, 90, 91, 103, 121, 145, and 147 are some of my favorites for reading to patients. I believe the entire Bible is the Word of God, but I am sure you will agree that some portions will be much more appropriate in a given situation than others are. There is a Psalm for just about every occasion but some entire Psalms, and some portions of others, will probably not be what your patient needs to hear from you at a given time. Do some studying and preparation. Again, your main task is probably not to teach the patient, but rather to encourage her. Good encouragement requires preparation on your part, just as good teaching does. Just as you probably would not go to the pulpit without some preparation, we should not neglect to prepare for a one-on-one visit either.

If you are able, you might want to sing songs that your patient is likely to recognize. I keep a cheat sheet with the words of some good, familiar hymns and songs that I can sing a Capella. Again, be sure to pray for your patient. Remember that you are speaking to the Lord, who knows all about this patient and loves her far more than you and I ever could. It is wonderful to affirm God's love and promises in your prayer. I try, however, not to preach in my prayers. I try to always have a Bible with me, but I also find it is helpful to have some favorite verses memorized. It is also helpful to have at least a few familiar longer passages memorized, such as Psalm 23, the Beatitudes (Matthew 5:3-10) and the Lord's Prayer.

A patient who is confused

I can still remember when visiting with a confused person was a little disconcerting, or even scary, for me. Over the years, I have become very much at home with confused and even with somewhat psychotic people; the biggest key here is listening. What a surprise! I hope you don't get tired of me talking to you about listening. The confused person will probably not be as ready or willing to listen to you as a well-oriented person would be. You, however, can conceivably listen to the confused patient just as well as you can listen to the well-oriented patient. It is important to try to listen to confused people because listening to anyone shows that you care about that person. A confused person might well be helped simply by seeing that you care for him.

I remember one particular responsibility we had as chaplain interns and residents in the hospital. Whoever happened to be the chaplain on call on a Sunday morning had the duty of going to the psych floor and putting on a "church service" there. The patients expected it and would revolt if it did not happen. The first time or two that I did this, it was more than a little bit scary for me. Most of the people in the unit were there because they really needed to be there. They were adults who were verbal and usually ambulatory (walking around). I was not given much guidance as to what to do, but this is what I learned to do. I would show up with very little agenda and introduce myself as the on-call chaplain. There were always about 15 to 30 eager participants waiting for me to meet their needs. We had to have some singing, so I asked if we had any special requests. If someone really wanted a song that I did not know, they had the opportunity to lead the song. If no one else knew the song, we had an opportunity for a solo. Some of the participants were very talented. Some were not. Often participants wanted me to know who they were. I met a lot of famous people, whom I thought had died a long time ago. The most popular famous people were Jesus and Mary. We never had two competing Jesus impersonators on the same day, though. Thinking back, I suppose that is a good thing, but it would have been interesting.

I soon found myself really enjoying my trips to the psych floor to hold the Sunday service. I never knew who would show up, or what would happen, but I prayed before and during the service, and Jesus really was always there. I would usually have two or three possible passages picked out for the main message. The crowd, the music, and the Spirit always showed me the right direction to take the service. Looking back, those experiences were great training and preparation for the work that I continue to do as a chaplain. Visiting with one or two very confused people now does not seem to be such a great challenge, after frequently ministering to a large room full of very confused people.

All confusion is different. Even the same patient can present various kinds of confusion from one visit to the next. I am not a psychologist, but I can listen. Each of us can show that we care. We can also see and hear if a patient seems to be anxious or very sad. This is important because I report to medical personnel when it appears that a patient is fearful or unnaturally sad. You, too, can always respectfully report such observations to family members and to the patient's nurse or physician. There are no HIPAA rules against reporting your own observations to the medical folks. Please do not try to make medical decisions for them, though.

While it is important to listen to very confused or psychotic people, please do not believe everything that they tell you. I remember well a lesson I learned on the psych floor, early in my time as a chaplain intern. I was asked to visit a patient who was known by all to be very anxious, but I came to realize that she was also paranoid. As the patient spoke to me, she began to tell me how other patients in the ward were plotting against her. Next, she told me that the professional staff was also plotting against her. I soon realized that, given enough time, this patient was going to be thinking, and saying, that I was plotting against her. I got a little concerned when the patient said something about calling 911 to tell the authorities what was "really going on" on the psych floor. This patient was psychotic but was also well spoken and quite convincing. After visiting with her at some length, I spoke to the psychiatrist in charge, telling him what the patient said. He gave a little smile and let me know that patients in psych wards all over the city call 911 with some regularity. The 911 centers know which calls are coming from psych wards and they don't take such calls very seriously. They know that these callers are already under professional care. When the good doctor explained this to me, I felt great relief, and also felt pretty silly.

Dementia is a general term covering many kinds of reduced cognitive ability and confusion. Alzheimer's is just one fairly common disorder causing dementia. People with any kind of dementia are still the same person that they were years before, but we cannot communicate with them in the same ways that we used to. They cannot function as they once did, but they are still worthy of our respect, our love, and our care. Most commonly, confusion will increase over time, although sometimes it will decrease a little for a brief period. There are many patients who show what is commonly called "sundowners." This refers to their tendency to become significantly more confused in the evening hours, or even in late afternoon. With those patients, it is best to visit only during the morning hours if you really want to connect with them in any way. Other patients are never alert before noon. People can be very different, and a patient's level of confusion is not usually predictable. When moments of increased clarity present themselves, enjoy them, and just be thankful that you were there.

Many nurses have been taught to try to "redirect" patients when they show that they are not oriented to time or place or person. Redirecting the patient — telling her that it is afternoon, not morning, or telling the patient that they are in a nursing facility, not in the home where they lived for 40 years — is only occasionally and temporarily effective. Without getting too complicated here, I will tell where I have arrived on this issue. I work hard not to lie to my patients. I do, however, try to meet my patient where he is. I have found it is almost always okay to redirect a patient to the correct time of day, but I am rarely eager to redirect my patient to the right year. If I find a patient very happy in the 1950s, I let him stay there. I even join him there in conversation if that seems appropriate. If the patient thinks he is still at home in Florida, I don't correct him by telling him he is in a nursing facility in a different state, unless there is a really good reason to do so. If the 90-year-old patient speaks as though his mother is still living, I don't stop him and tell him that his mother is dead. I listen to his story and encourage him to tell me more about what his mother means to him.

Orientation to a person is usually the final stronghold, the last thing lost into confusion. I will never forget going to visit a patient in a nursing home and clearly hearing a conversation on the other side of a curtain in the same room. The man tearfully said to his wife, "I am your husband, don't you even remember who I am?" Dementia is usually very heartbreaking to loved ones because it can radically change or even extinguish a relationship long before the loved one dies.

You may want to report to your patient's nurse or physician if your patient appears full of fear or seems to be depressed. Sometimes medicines can help with these issues. And again, 1 Thessalonians 5:14 tells us to, "... comfort the fainthearted, uphold the weak, be patient with all." We do this mostly with kind, caring words. We can tell the patient that the Lord loves him and is always watching over him. We can affirm the patient, if possible, recalling his faith, his good deeds, and his love and kindness to others in past days. We can assure him that the Lord understands, the Lord loves him, and the Lord is still in control. Did you notice that I repeated the part about the Lord loving the patient? Please always feel free to repeat that yourself also.

A patient or family member who is angry

Anger is a fairly common emotion. Almost all of us get angry occasionally, and it seems to me that people today feel free to express their anger much more than they used to. That is not always good. I want to consider here what we should do when the people we minister to get angry? There is a theological question that comes up: Is anger always bad or wrong? I am not going to solve this somewhat complex issue here, but let's just listen to a few passages that speak to the question. Proverbs 29:22 tells us, "An angry man stirs up strife, and a furious man abounds in transgression." I hope we remember James 1:19a, but let's read it again, along with the rest of verse 19 and verse 20. "So then, my beloved brethren, let every man be swift to hear, slow to speak, slow to wrath; for the wrath of man does not produce the righteousness of God." Ephesians 4:26 & 27 says to us, "Be angry, and do not sin, do not let the sun go down on your wrath, nor give place to the devil."

My own simple summary is that anger is, in itself, not always sinful. Anger, however, holds a lot of dangerous potential. It leads the charge, and then a lot of sinful behavior follows. We should strive to be in control of our own emotions, even as we recognize that many other people are not in control of theirs. Anger is definitely an emotion that can lead any one of us into trouble, especially if in the heat of this emotion we act without thinking or praying first. This is important because I want to consider how to respond to people who are angry. We do not want to confront their anger with anger of our own. That just leads to an escalation of the anger. That's how the world has given us bar room brawls, riots, and wars. We know there is a better way.

In the hospital, I was confronted with angry family members more often than I was with angry patients. When a code green was called out over the hospital speaker system, the on-call chaplain and the security guys were all to respond to the location named. I will share with you here the very simple procedure that I was taught. Sometimes I arrived before the security guards could get to the scene. The usual situation involved some man, or some lady, angrily shouting about something. When I arrived, I would try to get this person's attention and calmly tell him something like, "Hey man, (or "Sir', or "Ma'am") you really sound upset. I want to hear what you have to say." Then I would actively listen. You see, no one else was really listening to the angry, shouting man. But that is what most angry, shouting people really want. They shout because they want to be heard. When the shouter sees that someone actually wants to listen, they often calm down and present their case rationally. This is at least part of what Proverbs 15:1 is telling us. "A soft answer turns away wrath, but a harsh word stirs up anger." This principle works in hospitals, nursing homes, and private homes. I really have not tried it out in bars and I would definitely not try it in a full-blown riot, but seriously, be cautious with angry people. Please do not think that this little bit of wisdom will somehow turn you into a person who can calm every angry soul and stop every fight. Proverbs 26:17 gives us a blunt warning. "He who passes by and meddles in a quarrel not his own is like one who takes a dog by the ears." Just last week, I heard a story on the news. A well-minded person tried to stop a fight on the street that night. The innocent man, who tried to help bring peace, was stabbed and killed by one of the two men who were trying to fight each other. If you think about it, you have probably heard of similar incidents. Police officers are highly trained and equipped to handle such situations, but these are dangerous for them as well. We need to recognize our own limitations and make wise decisions.

Now, back to what we should try to do in situations where anger invades. Plan A is to actively listen to the angry person. Plan B should always be to have a way of escape in case Plan A does not work. I remember a recent home visit that we were told was potentially dangerous. An adult son of one of our patients had been angry and threatening during an earlier nursing visit. I met one of our nurses in the street, not far from the house. We don't have security personnel when we visit in private homes, but we do have the ability to call 911, and so do you. The nurse and I agreed on a code word — "focused." The nurse would simply leave the house and literally drive away in her Ford Focus if I said the word, "focused." I would use the code word if I sensed that something dangerous was about to happen. I can assure you, I was going to leave soon after the nurse did if things got to that point. As it turned out, there were no problems that day, but at least we had a simple escape plan. Yes, I prayed too.

I will add one other note that further explains what I just told you. We had a security expert come and speak to our staff a year or two ago. The one thing that I remember him saying was that the most important safety device we have available to us is that small voice of warning we sometimes hear in our heads. He told us that if we are about to get in an elevator with someone we don't know, and the small voice says, "Do not get in the elevator with him", then we had better listen and not get in the elevator. Listening to that small voice was the only thing that kept my wife and me from getting robbed on a recent vacation. It's very important to pray, but it is also very important to listen.

A patient who is actively dying
Most of the time when a patient is actively dying, he or she is responding little if any to those around her. The same basic guidelines apply here as you read under the situation heading – A patient who is minimally responsive or nonresponsive. I want to offer here some additional thoughts and observations. Many of these are regarding friends and family members. I would also like to mention a few of the signs we see when a patient is nearing death.

Often a large circle of friends and family gather when a patient is reported to be nearing death. Here is a simple truth. As good as medical professionals may be at discerning when a patient is actively dying, even they do not have the ability to know for sure when the time of death will come. I can remember going to a hospital ER years ago where the family, in a moment of panic, had taken their father, who had really hoped his death would come peacefully at home. Four or five family members were there, as were a hospice RN and I. The ER Physician rather quickly assessed the patient and told the family that he thought the patient would probably die within 24 hours. I whispered to the nurse, "He will be gone in 20 minutes." She nodded and we were right. At least the family and some caring professionals were all there with him as he died. Please realize that no one knows for sure when death will come. Experience teaches us a lot, but I have seen many times when the nurses and doctors all agreed that a patient was certainly going to die very soon and the patient somehow hung onto life for a few more days.

The patients who have most often amazed me with their strength and endurance are the "ladies in their eighties." We do not know when death will occur, and that is okay, even when it interferes with our own tightly organized schedules. I often include these words in the required notes I write after each visit, "Tried to help family members reflect on the the unknown timing of patient's coming death."

Sometimes it seems that the reason why some people vigorously hang onto life, beyond all expectations, is because there is some unresolved issue in their lives. Our main job, as I see it, is to do what we can to be sure that the patient is at peace with God; before he dies. I also make it my goal to try and help the patient be sure he is at peace with his family, and even with himself. Again, <u>our main tools, along with prayer, are listening to the patient and then sharing God's Word in a wise, loving and discerning way</u>. Remember that even when the patient may be too weak to speak to you, he may still, hopefully, be able to speak to the Lord in his heart.

Years of observation have seemed to show me, and medical professionals have told me this as well, that the human body is physically programmed to keep on fighting for life with every bit of strength that it has, until there is just no more. Death can still come very quickly, however. Heart attacks, strokes, and pulmonary issues can bring a very sudden end to life. I have also seen many occasions when it at least seemed that a patient chose the time at which they would die. Just as an example, several years ago I was with a lady in the hospital who was actively dying and minimally responsive. Over a period of hours, all of her children were arriving, and then staying at her bedside. There was, however, one son who was a merchant marine, who was at sea at that time. A ship to shore connection was managed. A phone was held to the patient's ear and the son said goodbye to his mom. Barely a minute after the brief phone call ended, the patient died peacefully. I know that story sounds like a script from a melodrama on television, but I was in the room to see it and hear it myself.

We have also seen occasions when the patient seemed to wait until the one moment when all of the family members were out of the room. I sometimes tell family members who are present for the passing of their loved one that they have received a rare gift. It seems that more often death occurs, in one of many ways, at a time when family members are not present. Good palliative care increases the odds that the family will be able to be present with their loved one, both before and at the time of death. I personally hope my loved ones will be close by when I leave this mortal body behind. We are not in control of the timing, but the Lord. In Psalm 31:15 David wrote, "My times are in your hand."

There are some common physical signs we see in a patient that indicate he is actively dying. Skin color usually becomes paler. Nail beds and lips will frequently fade and sometimes even take on a bluish color. Sometimes there is a gray or ashen appearance to the face no matter what the natural skin color is. A dying patient will usually relax his jaw and eyelids completely sometime before he dies. This means that many times the mouth will open wide as the jaw just seems to hang there. Some people keep their eyes closed. Some have their eyes half open or even fully open, but they stop blinking, and the non-focusing eyes can take on a glazed appearance. It can be very informative to watch the patient's breathing, as it may become very rapid. If I see this before a doctor or nurse arrives, I tell the medical folks that the patient seems to be working very hard to breathe. Liquid pain medicine and usually some type of anti-anxiety medicines are often given according to the doctor's direction. Oxygen is sometimes delivered to the patient through a cannula (a little clear oxygen tube to the nostrils) or sometimes with a mask that covers mouth and nose. Oxygen at this point is often more for comfort than anything else. Breathing may be rapid, but it almost always slows down eventually to a slower than normal rate before death comes. Even when the breaths are slow and becoming shallow, the patient will usually be using all of his rib-cage to breathe, sort of like you and I do after running up a hill. Often we see what is called apnea. This is observed as pauses in the breathing rhythm that can last a few seconds or up to 30 seconds or more. Such pauses seem to be longer than they really are. Many times, observers think that the patient has died, and then he takes another big breath. Sometimes, just before death occurs, the patient will purse his lips a little and breathe a few very short and shallow breaths. Sometimes the patient will breathe one or two final deep breaths, then no more. When you have seen this once you will recognize most of these signs. When you have watched dozens of people die, you will still continue to learn and be amazed, and sometimes surprised.

Sometimes a patient who has been put on a ventilator is determined to be terminally ill, with no real chance of recovery. The family and the physicians come to the conclusion that their terminally ill patient should be taken off of the ventilator. Patients are put on ventilators for a variety of reasons, and the hope is always that there will be some kind of recovery so that the patient can eventually be able to breathe on his own again. When there is no recovery, and the patient's prognosis becomes more and more hopeless, then a difficult decision has to be made. Many times I have been asked to be present when a patient is taken off of his ventilator. Several of these times, I have also been present when the physician or physicians explained the circumstances to the family. In such cases, I normally ask the family if they have understood what the doctor has told them, and ask if they have any more questions for the doctor. This is such a sad and difficult and in some ways, unnatural situation. The ventilator has extended the patient's life, but it and other tools have not been able to cure or rescue the patient. It is sort of like putting support structures around an old collapsing building. The support structures may help for a while, but sometimes it is just not enough. The building continues to deteriorate and there is just no more that can be done. One is then in the awful situation where one has to remove the support structures, knowing that the building will then completely collapse.

The removal of the breathing tube, hence the disconnecting of a patient from his ventilator is usually done in an intensive care unit of a hospital. Sometimes the patient dies within minutes of being extubated and sometimes such a patient amazes us and continues to live for hours or even days. When all of this is done properly, the patient will die naturally, but he will have sufficient medication in his system to prevent him from feeling agony and distress. In some ways, such a death is more difficult for the family than most other deaths. It is good for us to know and understand the situation, and be able to assure the family members that they did all that they could do for their loved one.

A death call at home

Many times you and I will be called by family members, telling us that their loved one has just died. If they are calling to tell you this, they most likely want you to come and be with them, even if they do not specifically tell you that. They may say, "Please come." Get there as quickly as you safely can. They may call you and say, "Oh' don't feel like you have to come." Get there quickly, just the same. Because they called you, they really want you to be there. If you get word from others and you make the call to the family, listen to whatever they request of you and go if they ask you to.

We have spoken a little bit already about a death in the ER or other areas of a hospital. A death at home has its own peculiarities. When a patient dies at home, it is usually the case that the person was a hospice patient. In such cases, the family will often be asked by a nurse, "Do you want our chaplain to come, or do you have a pastor or someone else you can call?" If you are making visits with a terminally ill patient and his family, hopefully, you can tell them that you are reachable and that they can call you in case of emergency, and in particular at the time of the patient's death. Here are some typical events that happen after the death of a hospice patient at home.

Family members often show a great display of emotion at, or just after, the time of death. This can happen even when the death has long been anticipated, and even when the family has seemed "fully prepared" for what was coming. Ideally, you would have been present for the death itself, which can be a beautiful, amazing experience. It is very good when the patient passes peacefully with no signs of pain or distress. Most deaths I have seen are this way.

When I am there with a family at the time of their loved one's death, I often say a brief prayer of thanks to God for His grace and His wonderful promises in regard to eternity. I usually try to pray with and for the family, before the funeral directors arrive. It can become a very emotional time when the patient's body is taken out of the home. This seems to be even more difficult when the deceased has lived for a long time in their home. I almost always stay with the family until after the funeral directors have come and gone. It usually takes them anywhere from 30 minutes to over an hour to arrive after they get the call to come.

I try to know the names of the closest relatives of the deceased who are present in the home. Then when the funeral directors arrive, I try to meet them at the door or even just outside the door. I tell them who I am, and my role. Then introduce the funeral directors to the closest relatives of the deceased. They appreciate it when they don't have to come in the house and ask "who is who."

In the state where I typically minister, the funeral director will need to ask the closest relative for permission to embalm the body of the deceased. This is necessary if they are going to have a traditional funeral with a viewing of the body.

At the time of this writing, about half of all deceased persons are now being cremated in the United States. In some European countries, the great majority of people choose cremation. Before cremation can take place, a physician will need to sign the original death certificate and close relatives will have to give their permission. If the deceased is to be cremated, the departure of the body from the home takes on an even greater importance, as this would most likely be the last occasion for the family to actually see their loved one's body. Some families actually choose to embalm, have a viewing and then have the body cremated afterward.

Another note about the funeral directors who come. Sometimes they are morticians who are contracted by the funeral home to come and "receive" the body, taking it then to the funeral home or mortuary. Unless your area has a large number of funeral homes, you might actually get to know the people who come to pick up the bodies. It seems like most of the ones that I run into already know me, and they are glad to see us there supporting the family. Sometimes only one person comes, sometimes two. More and more, women serve in this role. You might possibly be asked to assist in physically carrying the body of the deceased around a narrow corner of a hallway from the bedroom to the gurney. I have a few times helped carry a body down a staircase. In most situations, we encourage family members to wait in another room while the body is lifted from the bed to the gurney. If I am not needed to assist, I want to be with the family members at this time.

Closing thoughts:

This has been a human attempt to impart to you as much as I could in these few pages. Obviously, the only words that are inspired here are those quoted from the Bible. I wish I could have said more and said it better. I hope that I have not said too much that will offend. Mostly I hope that I have not erred from the truth, nor encouraged others to do so in any way.

Please pray as you go. Please ask God to help you to love those you minister to. Please expect people to disappoint you, and expect God to amaze you.

Beloved, let us love one another, for love is of God; and everyone who loves is born of God and knows God.

He who does not love does not know God, for God is love.

In this the love of God was manifested toward us, that God has sent His only begotten Son into the world, that we might live through Him.

In this is love, not that we loved God, but that He loved us and sent His Son to be the propitiation for our sins.

Beloved, if God so loved us, we also ought to love one another.

1 John 4:7-11

VII

APPENDIX

Four steps to overcoming fear

1. Freely acknowledge your own **Weakness** and limitations.
This may sound rather counter-intuitive, but it is essential and foundational. God is not looking to use people who are self-confident. He is looking for people who are God-confident. (Read the story of King Asa in 2 Chronicles 14:2, 9-12; then 16:1-9)

It appears to be the natural way of men and women, young or mature, to be working toward self-confidence. Many people seem to achieve this, but God is not impressed. Men will often follow one who is self-confident, but God clearly wants to use people who place their confidence in Him.

In Paul's second letter to the Corinthians, he told this church about his personal struggle with some unnamed disease or weakness. Paul said this ailment was intended by God to keep him from being "exalted above measure." (2 Corinthians 12:7) In verse 8, Paul said "Concerning this thing I pleaded with the Lord three times that it might depart from me." Then comes verse 9, "And the Lord said to me, "My grace is sufficient for you, for My strength is made perfect in weakness."

Paul closes verse 10 with the words, "For when I am weak, then I am strong." Please, please get ahold of the meaning of 2 Corinthians 12:9. God works with human weakness. God clearly disdains the illusions of human strength and pride. The statement, "God resists the proud, but gives grace to the humble" is found in Proverbs 3:34; James 4:6 and a third time in 1 Peter 5:5.

For a good study on pride, humility and boldness focused on one individual, try reading the last 3 chapters of Luke, the last chapter of John and the first five chapters of Acts, focusing throughout these chapters on the words, actions, and heart of the Apostle Peter. Notice how this man acted rashly and responded with fear when he was still walking in pride. After he was humbled through his own failure, this same man seemed to have no more issues with fear. He boldly preached, and faithfully led others.

Now a small personal story... I have always been a rather tall, skinny guy who wished he was bigger and stronger. I have spent countless hours lifting weights with little visible results. Several years ago I was getting some physical therapy done on an injured shoulder. In the same room, another rather thin fellow was also getting some kind of therapy. He was clearly trying to muster up his own self-confidence, or at least was trying to encourage others to think more of him. He told his female physical therapist a story of confronting some other young man and then told the therapist, "I'm a lot stronger than I look."

The minute I heard this, it grabbed ahold of my conscience. I said, "Lord, I hope I have never said those juvenile, arrogant words." But I knew I had. And I know I have said other such things to try to somehow get others to think more of me. That day, I got a picture of just how foolish such words and actions sound and look. I can only imagine how foolish such boastings appear to God.

So what do we do with this important point? Just relax a little here. Accept the way God made you. He knew what He was doing, and He still does. You don't have to be bullet-proof. Your friends will still accept you when they find out that you are not so strong. They probably already know anyway. God is the ultimate strong. God knows you best because He made you. He loves you best, too.

2. Remember and affirm **God's presence** with you.
We often read about fear in those whom God calls to serve Him. In Jeremiah Chapter 1, we have the account of God calling the young Jeremiah into a ministry of being God's prophet. Here it is. God speaks with Jeremiah in

chapter 1:5-8. "Before I formed you in the womb I knew you; before you were born I sanctified you; I ordained you a prophet to the nations." Then said I: "Ah, Lord God! Behold, I cannot speak, for I am a youth."

But the LORD said to me: "Do not say, 'I am a youth,' for you shall go to all to whom I send you, and whatever I command you, you shall speak. <u>Do not be afraid of their faces, for I am with you to deliver you," says the LORD."</u>

Another clear passage in the Old Testament is found in Isaiah 41:10: "Fear not, for I am with you; be not dismayed, for I am your God. I will strengthen you, Yes, I will help you; I will uphold you with My righteous right hand."

It sounds a little strange to us today, but you know that throughout the Scriptures, both in the Old and New Testaments, we are told to *fear* God. There are actually many dozens of passages we could reference here. One I like is found in Psalm 5:7: "But as for me, I come into Your house in the multitude of Your mercy; in fear of You I will worship toward Your holy temple. Lead me, O LORD, in Your righteousness because of my enemies; Make Your way straight before my face."

Psalm 5:11-12 speaks of confidence in God's protection over us: "But let all those rejoice who put their trust in You; let them ever shout for joy, because You defend them; let those also who love Your name Be joyful in You. For You, O LORD, will bless the righteous; with favor You will surround him as with a shield."

Remembering God's presence with us, and fearing Him, we need not fear any other.

Psalm 27:1 is a great verse to hold in our hearts.

"The LORD is my light and my salvation; whom shall I fear? The LORD is the strength of my life; of whom shall I be afraid?"

Without a doubt, the greatest way to remind ourselves of God's presence and protection is to pray. The third shortest verse in the Bible comes right after the second shortest. It is 1 Thessalonians 5:17. We all know this one, but none of us do it. "Pray without ceasing."

Please do not try to explain this verse away with some literary tricks. Here's how I see this. As long as I am awake and not super focused on something very intense, like a 60 second run through a fast autocross course, I am always thinking, and usually talking to myself. Since I am told to pray without ceasing, should I not just share all my thoughts consciously with the Lord? The beautiful Psalm 139 makes it poetically clear that God knows all of our words and thoughts, and He is ever with us to lead us. Should we not invite the Lord into our every thought and plan? Should we not turn to Him first, at every hint of danger or anxiety? Now, I realize this is easier said than done. We so easily drift off and away in our thoughts. We can work on this though, and we can invite the Lord to help us to do what he has already told us to do.

So try to pray without ceasing. Remember the Lord is ever-present, ever-understanding and as gracious as He is powerful.

Psalm 147, verse 10 always makes me laugh, just before verse 11 encourages me.
"He does not delight in the strength of the horse; He takes no pleasure in the legs of a man. The LORD takes pleasure in those who fear Him, in those who hope in His mercy."

3. Another very helpful "strategy" is to **focus on the one you are dealing with**.
In Philippians 4, Paul was trying to teach this wonderful church not to worry. That is a great lesson for us all. In the well-known verse, Philippians 4:6, we read that we should be praying instead of worrying. But the Lord inspired Paul to take this a step further. The same step helps us not only to conquer worry, but also fear. Often there is indeed no difference between worry and fear. In verse 8, Paul tells us all positively what to think about. You and I know that, when someone tells us not to think about something, we almost automatically think of the very thing we are told not to think about. Likewise, if we try to just get a particular song out of our head, it

can be very difficult to do. The best strategy seems to be, to replace the one annoying song with a different song of our own choosing. Likewise, thoughts of worry and or fear can be pushed out of our minds when they are displaced by thoughts of our own choosing. Paul told the Philippians to think on things that are true and noble and just and pure and lovely.

Paul was teaching in regards to somewhat different problems than I am trying to address here, but the principle of displacing anxious thoughts with better ones is basically the same. I want you to focus your thoughts on the person you are dealing with, and on that person's situation, instead of focusing on yourself.

You know that many people cannot seem to take a good, natural picture when they "pose" in front of a camera. They are focused (no pun intended) on themselves and how they might look to others. These people always seem to end up with a fake, goofy expression on their faces for such pictures. But if you can sneak up on them when they are focused on something or someone else, you can capture this person with a natural expression that is not at all posed.

So often the things that we need to be pushed out of our minds are the constant thoughts about me, myself and I. What is going to happen to me? What do they think about me? I don't really want to be here right now. I am so embarrassed. I don't know what to say. I am afraid.

When we are focused on someone else or something else, we are more likely to be natural. We then tend to be much more real and more authentic, simply because we are not focused on ourselves. We are then less likely to be thinking about what we might look like to others. So we will not tend to be "afraid of their faces." We will have much less problem with fear. We will do a lot less "posing," if we can ***simply focus on the one to whom we are trying to minister***.

A great way to focus on the other person is to begin by praying for him or her, and also by trying to imagine what they are going through. Then ask some kind, gentle questions and listen with a kind heart.

How to focus? Pray for the one you are communicating with. Listen prayerfully to her.

After acknowledging your own weakness and remembering God's powerful presence with you, and after focusing on the one you are dealing with, instead of on yourself; we come to one more spiritual step.

4. It is time to just **Jump in the pool**.
I probably became most aware of my fear of other people's disapproval while working in the hospital ER, but this fourth lesson I learned through a visit in the ICU. I had written a verbatim about a visit with a family gathered around their dying mother, who was lying on a hospital bed in a small, crowded room.

Working with families of patients in the ICU often involved hours and sometimes even days of watching, waiting and anticipating. This was fairly early in my time as a chaplain intern in a local hospital. Martha (as we will call this lady) was in grave condition; we were told that she was going to die, but no one knew exactly when or how it would happen. Seven or eight family members were crowded into the room, all grieving with tears and anguish.

I wrote in my verbatim that it was like they were all wading around in some kind of a pool of grief while I was just standing there on the side of the pool, not knowing how to begin or what to do. My CPE supervisor's eyes lit up when he heard this, and he replied, "You were there standing on the edge of the pool. Why not just jump in the pool with them!"

I know it sounds simple, but it was a great moment. I still remember what I learned that day, and for months, many of us interns frequently used the expression with one another, "It's time to just jump in the pool."

That picture has a beautiful sense of self-abandon. It's another picture of setting self aside in order to focus on another person or even a group of people. The application from this story actually became quite frequent for me in the ICU. I ended up "jumping in the pool with so many families there. This same principle has become an almost daily thing for me in working with terminally ill patients and their families.

Just jumping in is also an attitude of simple boldness. I do not mean recklessness, but so often we hesitate, just looking for an excuse not to jump in quite yet, even when we know we should. Delay can lead to more delay, and then the visit never gets made, the job never gets done, the number is never dialed and the message is not yet sent. Anyone can study hard, reading books on how to swim. But that could never bring the actual accomplishment.

It is time to kick off your flip-flops and jump in the pool. As we looked to Jeremiah earlier, I would like to hear the Lord in chapter 1:7-8 one more time.

"Do not say 'I am a youth (or too old, or too shy or too untrained), for you shall go to all to whom I send you. And whatever I command you, you shall speak. Do not be afraid of their faces, for I am with you to deliver you, says the LORD."

Marsha's Story

I was hurrying away at the end of a bereavement visit with Marsha that had lasted over an hour. Marsha had told me about working on completing the many insurance and business transactions related to the death of her husband John. Marsha and John had been married for 64 years, and John had died less than three weeks before. On the day that John died, I had gotten there about 30 minutes after he passed. As soon as I got there, Marsha had said to me, "I have never felt such profound loneliness." Now Marsha was standing in her front doorway, and I was halfway down the stone steps leading to the circular driveway.

Marsha said, "I know you don't have time to hear this now, but I remembered something that happened a long time ago that has helped me to face what I'm going through now."

I started to agree that I had to leave right away, but instead, I stopped and asked Marsha to tell me her story.

Marsha said, "John and I were in Paris, traveling with a tour group. We had some time for ourselves, and we decided to take the Paris subway to the American Express office. We wanted to change our leftover English pounds into French francs. On our way, we had to change trains in a crowded station, with hundreds of people pushing and moving in all directions. Then I looked up and could not see John. I began to feel a sense of panic, looking everywhere, but as far as I could see, John was nowhere to be found. I suddenly felt completely lost. I was alone in a city of several million people. I had absolutely no money with me and I realized I did not even know the name of the hotel where we were staying. I only knew that it had a French name. I had never felt so lost and alone.

Then it occurred to me; we had been on our way to the American Express Office. I had a pretty good idea of how we were supposed to get there, so I decided to press on alone to where we had both been headed. It was not easy and I was anxious as I made my way along. And then, after many minutes that seemed like years, I made it to the place that had been our common goal. I hurried quickly to the door. John was already there, and he stepped out to meet me. He had even changed the money already and now, suddenly, everything was perfect and wonderful. We were in Paris, and I was together with John."

Marsha realized that once before, many years ago, she had been rudely separated from her beloved husband. This time the separation would be longer, but Marsha knew that she would be together with John again. Until then, she would continue to make her way, heading for what had always been their common goal. Marsha and John both had the hope of heaven in their hearts. Marsha has now passed on also, leaving this place of mortality behind her. I can now easily imagine them both together with their Lord and Savior, in the Heavenly City where the Lamb of God is the Light.

ENDNOTES

1   Alan D. Wolfelt, <u>Healing a Friend's Grieving Heart</u> (Companion Press, 2001), 13.
2   Ibid., *14.*
3   Ibid., 15.

Printed in the United States
By Bookmasters